Raising a Happy Dog

Akshay Mahendru

Published by Wyzr Content Pvt. Ltd.

ISBN (Paperback): 978-81-964817-5-9
ISBN (Hardback): 978-81-964817-9-7
ISBN (eBook): 978-81-964817-1-1

Editors: Yashraj Sharma, Amlan Chakravarty, Arpit Shandilya, Disha Dilip

Typeset in Adobe InDesign by Amlan Chakravarty

Cover by Syed Rizvi
Illustrations by DALL-E

Printed and bound by Gopsons Papers Pvt. Ltd.

First printing edition 2025

To all my furry friends I have met over the years, and to the ones I will meet in future.

Contents

1. Introduction

Back in 1995, my then 8-year-old brother brought a stray puppy home, intent on keeping it as a pet. As a family, we loved animals. We often fed the dogs in our neighbourhood and did our bit to shelter them during extreme heat or cold, both of which came around every year in Delhi.

But caring full-time for a pet wasn't something we thought we could do. Both my parents were working, and my brother and I were school boys who wouldn't be around half a day. It didn't seem like a great idea to adopt a pet in those circumstances.

But the look in that puppy's eyes was hard to ignore. I just couldn't get myself to abandon him. I suspect my parents felt the same. That's why when I announced that being the elder son, I would take the responsibility of raising the puppy; it didn't take too much convincing.

I didn't have any idea how I'd raise the puppy, but I believed that with the affection I had for him, I'd somehow figure it out.

But it was harder than I thought.

One day, the puppy began vomiting and had bloody diarrhoea. I was unsure of what to do. After asking some neighbours, I found a veterinary clinic about five kilometers from my house and rushed him there.

After a few rounds of checkups, the vet diagnosed him with *parvo*, a potentially fatal viral disease, and admitted him for treatment. I spent long, anxious hours at the clinic over the next week. But despite our efforts, we couldn't save him. We were all heartbroken, and my younger brother was inconsolable.

I felt terribly guilty because I was the one in charge. I had assured my parents and my brother that the puppy would be my responsibility.

As time went by, I realized that it wasn't just the devastating disease he contracted, but also our family's limited knowledge of puppy care that led to his demise. Today, I know that had we taken some basic precautions, we could have saved him.

Today, I know that having love and affection for a pet is a wonderful start, but not sufficient for the pet to live a healthy life. Knowledge and the right information are equally important.

That episode had a lasting impact on me, and my desire to do something good for pets and pet owners only grew with time. Incidentally, my father got into pet product trading, and through his work, I garnered more knowledge and insights about pet care and the industry at large.

In 2003, we opened our first "The Pet Point" store in Punjabi Bagh, Delhi, marking my official entry into the pet care industry. At the time of writing, we have grown to 14 stores across the NCR and Chandigarh, and interact with over 500 pets and pet parents every day through them. I have been fortunate to witness the evolution of not just this industry from close quarters, but also people's perceptions towards pets and parenting them.

Evolution of our perspective towards dogs

Initially, pet ownership was considered a hobby in India, with "pet parenting" emerging as a more recent phenomenon. Especially in metro cities, people initially kept dogs for security purposes. As nuclear families weren't prevalent then, the need for companionship was low. However, over time, people began to appreciate the warmth and companionship dogs offer beyond their primary role of providing security.

Previously, pet ownership was believed to be an expensive endeavour, suitable only for the affluent. Gradually, dogs transitioned from being predominantly security providers to status symbols. The rise of nuclear families and the increasing population of late-marrying migrant white-collar workers also contributed to dogs becoming a popular choice as pets. This resulted in an increase in the number of available breeds for prospective pet parents.

This trend was given a massive push by the Covid-19 lockdown. Those who had put off adopting a pet because of the limited time they spent at home didn't have that hurdle anymore. Moreover, people were forced to stay indoors, and children were not able to go out and play. Families and individuals turned to dogs to make their lives joyful even inside the confines of their homes.

Currently, estimates suggest that there are over 32 million pets in Indian households as of FY24. It accounts for lakhs of pet parents and over 3 million officially adopted dogs. It is also estimated that we are adding approximately 600,000 new pet adoptions every year. Consequently, the pet care industry has expanded alongside this growing interest in dog adoption. The Indian pet care industry is projected to be worth over $7.5 billion by FY28[1].

The attitude has also shifted from simply pet parenting to comprehensive pet care. Nowadays, dogs are not merely pets, but integral family members. This change has led pet owners to invest more in premium food, healthcare, and lifestyle products for their pets. A few years ago, it was standard to buy generic pet food and essential products. Now, pet owners pay attention to the ingredients in pet food, seek breed-specific supplements, and importantly, ask questions. It has become common for pet owners to understand the purpose and suitability of every product they consider for their pets.

When we opened our first store, we aimed to cater to all pet parent needs. We established a small clinic where a veterinarian could treat pets and a grooming area for busy parents to keep their pets well-groomed. Unfortunately, we didn't see any traction for these services for years.

Nowadays, such facilities have become the standard for new-age pet stores. This shift underscores the evolution of pet parenting and society's changing perspective towards it.

Why dogs?

It is no secret that dogs have solidified their status as man's best friend. Their unmatched popularity as pets comes with good reason.

Dogs, thanks to their unique traits and inherent nature, are seen as the epitome of companionship and loyalty. They have an unwavering devotion and loyalty that is hard to match. Their happy greetings and enthusiastic tail wags provide a constant source of affection and emotional support. They are known for their intelligence and trainability. Most breeds are eager to please and can be trained for various tasks, from basic obedience to impressive tricks. This mental stimulation is not only beneficial for the dog but also for the owner and helps build strong bonds between parents and the pet.

Moreover, dogs have a natural zest for life and love to be included in activities. They are great motivators for getting exercise and enjoying the outdoors. This active companionship promotes a healthy lifestyle, making the journey of health and fitness more enjoyable for pet owners.

Dogs, being naturally social creatures, can be excellent companions for people of all ages, providing a sense of security and often acting as a deterrent against intruders. This dual role of companion and protector is another reason why dogs are so beloved.

Lastly, the variety of breeds also plays a significant role in their popularity. With over 200 recognized breeds, dogs come in all shapes, sizes, and temperaments. This vast diversity allows people to find a dog that perfectly suits their lifestyle and living situation, whether it be a small apartment or a large farm.

While dogs may be the most popular choice, other pets also have their own charms. Cats, for instance, are independent and low-maintenance, offering companionship and purring comfort. However, they may not be as eager to please or suitable for those seeking an active companion.

Small animals like rodents and rabbits can be cute and cuddly, but they often have shorter lifespans and require specialized care. They may not offer the same level of interaction as a dog.

Fish can also make great pets. They can be calming and visually appealing, requiring minimal space. However, the interaction they offer is limited compared to dogs.

Ultimately, the best pet depends on your preferences and circumstances. If you crave an active, loyal friend who thrives on interaction and training, a dog might be the perfect match. The companionship and joy they bring into our lives are priceless. They are not just pets, but family, enriching our lives with their unconditional love, companionship, and unwavering loyalty.

Why I wrote this book

Life as a pet parent can be daunting at times, but having the right information can help us make informed decisions, even in tough times. In the era of social media, there's an abundance of content about pet parenting and dogs. However, useful information is scattered and drowned in the sheer volume of content.

The variety in dog breeds and sizes further complicates dog care, as their needs often depend on these factors. I've provided general guidelines, it's important to consider the variations for different breeds and sizes.

This book is my attempt to create a guide, a comprehensive resource that aims to address and answer an extensive range of questions a prospective dog owner might struggle with. It incorporates meticulously detailed sections dedicated to caring for a puppy right from the moment they set foot in your home, to a wide array of topics that include raising them right, pointers for their general well-being, traveling with them, socializing them effectively, and other vital aspects that contribute to their overall growth and development. Throughout the book, I've included real-life pet stories to emphasize the importance of every aspect of pet care.

Over the years, I've worked with countless pet owners, both new and experienced, and encountered all types of pet problems possible. Even though the industry has matured significantly over the last decade or so, no one has attempted to consolidate the right information in one place.

If a wagging tail brings you joy, this book provides everything you need to know before welcoming a puppy into your home. It equips you with essential information to smoothly embark on your journey as a dog parent and enjoy years of love and companionship with your furry friend.

Endnotes

1. Redseer Consulting, "Understanding India's evolving Petcare market", https://redseer.com/newsletters/from-kibble-to-care-understanding-indias-evolving-pet-care-market/

2. Is A Dog Right For You?

If you're thinking about getting a dog, congratulations! You're one step closer to joining the ranks of proud "pet parents." But before you start picking out collars or debating between "Fluffy" and "Sir Barks-a-lot" for a name, let's dig into this life-changing decision. Bringing a dog into your life is more than just adding a pet to your household. It's a choice that can reshape your daily routines, alter your social dynamics, and even change your perspective on life. As you contemplate this significant step, it's crucial to weigh both the joys and challenges of canine companionship.

First, let's talk about the incredible upsides of dog ownership. Imagine coming home after a long, tiring day at work. Instead of an empty house, you're greeted by a bundle of fur jumping around with excitement to see you. That's the magic of dogs – they have an uncanny ability to make you feel like the most important person in the world, even if you've only been gone for five minutes.

Over the years, running a pet products and supplies chain has given me the privilege of meeting people at different stages of their pet ownership journey. One particularly memorable incident stands out. A couple visited our store seeking to adopt a puppy after being married for seven years and struggling to conceive. The wife was heartbroken and nearing an emotional breakdown. Her husband suggested adopting a dog to help her cope with their situation. When we facilitated their adoption and they met their puppy for the first time in our store, the wife's eyes welled up with tears as the puppy snuggled against her. Through tear-filled eyes, she thanked us repeatedly. As they left the store with their new family member, we knew this was just the beginning of their journey filled with love, companionship, and joy.

While the above incident can be considered special for many reasons, dogs do have an extraordinary capacity to enhance our emotional and physical well-being. Their unwavering affection and loyalty can be a powerful antidote to stress, anxiety, and loneliness. The simple act of petting a dog has been shown to lower blood pressure and reduce stress hormones, while their need for regular exercise often translates into increased physical activity for their owners.

They possess a unique ability to break down social barriers, acting as natural icebreakers in various settings. Whether at the dog park, during neighborhood walks, or at pet-friendly establishments, dogs create opportunities for social interaction that might otherwise be missed.

Moreover, for families with children, dogs can be excellent teachers of empathy, responsibility, and consistent care. Through daily feeding routines, regular walks, and attentive care, children learn valuable life skills that extend far beyond pet ownership.

In a nutshell, dogs can be amazing catalysts for:

- Increased physical activity (say goodbye to a sedentary lifestyle)
- Stress reduction (nothing beats a cuddle session after a tough day)
- Social connections (dog parks are the new social hubs)
- Teaching responsibility to children (and sometimes adults too!)
- Unconditional love and companionship (your dog will never judge what you do)

While the benefits of dog ownership are numerous, it's essential to have a realistic understanding of the commitment involved. It's not all belly rubs and Instagram-worthy moments. Dogs require a significant investment of time, often necessitating adjustments to your daily routine and overall lifestyle.

From daily walks and feeding schedules to playtime and grooming, the time devoted to a dog's care can be substantial.

This commitment extends to considerations like travel plans, social engagements, and even work schedules, all of which may need to be adapted to accommodate your furry friend's needs. Some challenges you might face are:

- Early morning walks (rain, shine, or apocalyptic weather)
- Vet bills (because someone thought socks were part of a balanced diet)
- Constant cleaning (goodbye, pristine furniture; hello, lint rollers)
- Vacation planning (now featuring the phrase "Is it pet-friendly?")
- Lifestyle adjustments (spontaneous after-work drinks? Not so fast!)

Even when you're willing to accommodate lifestyle changes and are committed to raising a puppy, things may not work out as planned. It's crucial to have extensive conversations with experienced pet owners to truly understand what it takes. Take my friend Vaibhav's experience, for instance.

Fresh into his corporate career, Vaibhav attended a house party at his senior colleague's home. Upon meeting his senior's dog, he instantly fell in love with the idea of having his own pet. Though he asked his senior several questions about pet ownership, he mistakenly thought this brief conversation was sufficient research. Within weeks, he had adopted a puppy whom he named Ruby.

Initially, Vaibhav did everything right—regular vet checkups, creating a cozy space for the puppy, and providing proper food and treats. What he hadn't anticipated was how demanding his job would become. During his probation period, his workload was light, allowing him to return home early and spend time with Ruby.

However, his work responsibilities increased dramatically over the following months, forcing him to spend long hours at the office. Ruby's health and well-being deteriorated as she struggled with extended periods of solitude. When Vaibhav tried relocating her to his parents' home, it only made matters worse—his elderly parents couldn't keep up with Ruby's boundless energy. Ultimately, he had to give her up to another family. Despite our best intentions, some phases of life aren't suitable for pet ownership. It's crucial to recognize this reality and avoid putting ourselves and our beloved pets through challenging situations.

The Practical Aspects

Before you commit to dog ownership, ask yourself these questions:

1. **Do you have the time?** Dogs need exercise, training, and attention. They thrive on routine and companionship, which means you need to be consistent with their daily care. Can you dedicate at least an hour each day to your furry friend? This includes walks, playtime, and training sessions to ensure they are well-behaved and happy.
2. **Do you have any allergies?** This is a crucial consideration before bringing a dog into your home. Allergies to pet dander, saliva, or fur can cause a range of symptoms, from mild sneezing and itchy eyes to severe respiratory issues. It's important to evaluate whether you or any family members have known allergies to dogs. If you're unsure, consider spending time around dogs to see if any allergic reactions occur. Additionally, some breeds are considered hypoallergenic and may be a better fit for individuals

with allergies. However, it's essential to note that no dog breed is entirely hypoallergenic, and individual reactions can vary. Consulting with an allergist can provide personalized advice and help you make an informed decision.

3. **Can you afford it?** From food to vet bills, having dogs can be slightly expensive. Apart from the basics like food and regular vet check-ups, there are also unexpected costs such as emergency medical care, grooming, and pet insurance. Are you prepared for the financial commitment that includes all these aspects of pet care?
4. **Is your living situation suitable?** A Great Dane in a tiny studio apartment might not be the best idea. Consider your space and any rental restrictions. Some dogs need more room to roam and play, while others might be content in a smaller space. Additionally, check if your lease allows pets and if there are any breed or size restrictions.
5. **Are you ready for a long-term commitment?** Dogs can live 10-15 years or more. A friend of mine who has had pets for over 20 years now often says dogs are like 2-year-old kids who never grow up. This means they require ongoing care, love, and attention throughout their lives. Are you prepared for that level of commitment, knowing that you will need to provide for them in sickness and in health, through all stages of their lives?
6. **Can you handle the responsibility?** Dogs depend on us for everything. This includes feeding, exercising, grooming, and providing medical care. They also need emotional support and companionship. Are you ready to be the responsible party in this relationship, ensuring that your pet feels loved and secure at all times? This responsibility extends to training them properly so they can be good

canine citizens and fit well into your lifestyle and community.

7. **Are you fully prepared for the challenges that come with training a dog?** Dogs need a considerable amount of training irrespective of their breed in order to address any potential behavioral issues that may arise. This includes being ready to invest time, patience, and possibly seeking professional help if needed.
8. **Do you have a reliable support system in place?** There will be times when you might need assistance with your dog's care. This could involve friends, family, pet-sitters, or neighbors who can step in to help when you are unavailable or need a break.

The Alternatives

If you're on the fence, consider these alternatives to full-time dog ownership:

- **Fostering:** Experience the joys and responsibilities of dog ownership by temporarily taking in a dog in need. By fostering, you not only give a pup a safe and loving environment but also play a crucial role in their transition to a permanent home. This way, you can understand the daily tasks involved in pet care, including feeding, walking, and training. Additionally, fostering provides you with the opportunity to bond with the dog and see if you're ready for a long-term commitment. It's a fulfilling way to contribute to the well-being of animals and the community, as it helps shelters manage their resources and find forever homes for more dogs.
- **Dog-sitting:** Offer to watch friends' or family members'

dogs when they're away on vacation or business trips. This service not only helps them out by providing their pets with a safe and loving environment in their absence but also gives you the chance to spend time with different dog breeds and personalities. You can enjoy the company of various dogs, learning about their unique behaviors, preferences, and quirks. Additionally, dog-sitting can be a rewarding experience, offering you the opportunity to build a deeper bond with the animals and potentially even gain new skills in pet care and management.

- **Volunteer at a shelter:** Spend your free time volunteering at a local animal shelter. By dedicating a few hours each week, you'll get your dog fix, gain valuable experience in animal care, and contribute to the welfare of homeless dogs. This experience not only allows you to interact with a variety of dog breeds and personalities but also helps you understand their needs and behaviors better. Moreover, your efforts will make a significant difference in their lives, providing them with the attention and care they desperately need while they await permanent homes. Volunteering can also be a fulfilling way to connect with other animal lovers and build a supportive community.
- **Support Community dogs:** Take the initiative to care for and provide for community dogs in your residential area. Society's perspective towards community dogs has become more positive, with governmental laws now in place to protect and support caregivers. These dogs, often neglected and abused, can become aggressive due to mistreatment, leading to unfortunate mishaps. By caring for them, you can help improve their lives and reduce aggression, making the world a better place for them. This com-

passionate act not only satisfies your desire to have a pet but also contributes to the well-being of the community.

The Final Decision

Ultimately, deciding to get a dog is a deeply personal choice that involves careful consideration and reflection. It's a significant responsibility that should not be taken lightly, but for many people, the rewards and joys of dog ownership far outweigh the challenges and commitments involved.

So, is a dog right for you? Only you can answer that question after thoughtful consideration. But if you're ready for an adventure filled with love, laughs, and the occasional chewed-up slippers, dog ownership might just be the best decision you ever make. You'll find companionship, loyalty, and a special bond that few other experiences can offer.

Remember, a dog is for life, not just for Instagram or fleeting moments of fun. Choose wisely, love fully, and may your future be filled with wagging tails, wet-nosed kisses, and countless memories that will last a lifetime. Embrace the journey, and you'll discover that the love and joy a dog brings into your life are truly immeasurable.

3. Choosing A Perfect Match

Embarking on the journey to find your perfect canine companion is a bit like dating, minus the awkward small talk and overpriced coffee. It's an adventure filled with wagging tails, joyous barks, and the potential for a love story that'll last for years. This process involves not just an emotional connection but also careful consideration of various factors to ensure a harmonious and fulfilling relationship. But before you swipe right on the first pair of puppy dog eyes that make your heart melt, let's dive into the art and science of choosing your perfect match. Understanding the breed's characteristics, assessing your lifestyle, and considering the dog's needs are all crucial steps in this exciting quest. Whether you're looking for an energetic playmate, a loyal guard dog, or a gentle companion, these elements play a pivotal role in finding a dog that will truly complement your life. So, let's explore these aspects in detail to ensure your journey ends with the perfect furry friend by your side.

Know Thyself, Know Thy Dog

The key to a harmonious human-canine relationship isn't just about finding the cutest face in the doggy catalog (though I won't judge if that's a factor). It's about finding a dog whose personality, energy level, and needs align with your lifestyle. Are you a marathon runner looking for a four-legged training partner to keep you company on those long runs? Or are you more of a Netflix marathoner in search of a cuddle buddy who will snuggle up with you on the couch? Perhaps you're somewhere in between, seeking a dog who's up for both thrilling adventures and lazy Sundays lounging around.

Consider your living situation, work schedule, and social life. A high-energy Border Collie, for example, might not be the best fit for a small apartment and a 60-hour workweek. Similarly, a tiny Chihuahua might not be able to keep up with your daily 10-mile runs. It's essential to match the dog's energy level with your own to ensure both of you are happy and fulfilled.

Take Sarah, for example. She initially thought she wanted an Instagram-worthy Husky, drawn in by their wolf-like appearance and striking blue eyes. However, after honestly assessing her lifestyle – a demanding full-time job, a small apartment, and a love for sleep – she realized a Husky's high energy and need for extensive exercise wouldn't fit her life. She ended up adopting a laid-back Greyhound, finding her perfect match in a breed known as the "40 mph couch potato." The Greyhound's calm demeanor and moderate exercise needs were a perfect fit for Sarah's lifestyle, proving that sometimes the less obvious choice is the best one.

The bottom line is that building a fulfilling and lasting bond with your dog requires thoughtful consideration of your daily life and how a potential furry friend will fit into it. By doing so, you can create a happy, healthy relationship that brings joy and companionship for years to come.

The Great Debate: Adopt or Shop?

Now that you've done some soul-searching and have reflected deeply on your needs and desires, it's time to decide where to find your new best friend. The "adopt don't shop" mantra, which encourages people to adopt pets from shelters instead of buying them from breeders or pet stores, has gained significant popularity in recent years as more people become aware of the plight of homeless animals. However, the reality is a bit more nuanced, as there are various factors to consider, such as the type of pet that would best fit your lifestyle, the specific needs of different animals, and the ethical considerations involved in both adopting and purchasing pets.

The Case for Adoption

Adopting from a shelter or rescue organization can be an incredibly rewarding experience for many reasons. Not only are you giving a loving home to a dog in need, but you are also potentially saving a life that might not have had a bright future otherwise. Additionally, by adopting, you often get a dog that is already house-trained and has moved past the challenging puppy stage where they chew on everything in sight.

Shelters and rescue organizations usually have a wide variety of dogs available, ranging from purebreds to delightful and unique mutts. The staff at these places are often very knowledgeable and can help match you with the right dog based on your lifestyle, activity level, and personal preferences. They take the time to understand both the dogs and the prospective adopters to ensure a good fit, which can make the transition smoother for both you and your new pet.

Moreover, adoption fees at shelters and rescues are typically much lower than the cost of purchasing a dog from a breeder. These fees often include essential initial veterinary care, vaccinations, and spaying or neutering, which can save you a significant amount of money while ensuring that your new pet is healthy. By choosing to adopt, you not only enrich your own life but also contribute to the well-being of a dog in need, making it a mutually beneficial decision.

The Case for Reputable Breeders

On the other hand, choosing to go to a reputable breeder can be the right choice if you are looking for a specific breed, whether because of its temperament, size, or hypoallergenic coat.

One thing many people don't realize is that attitudes towards dogs have changed as more people started having pets. We encountered more pets and warmed up to them. In earlier days in India, dogs were mostly kept for security purposes or as status symbols. It was commonly understood that only rich people had dogs. Thankfully, with the increase in dog adoption, lifestyle changes, and the rise of nuclear families, the general population is now much more aware of what having a pet entails. So you can victimise breeders all you want, the rise of "Adopt, don't shop" happened because people realised dogs were more than just animals. They are family.

But that doesn't mean all breeders are doing what they should. Dog breeding has sadly become a business where illegal breeding, crossbreeding, and various inhumane practices are carried out to supply pups to eager families. It's very important to do your research and identify reputable and registered breeders who follow the law and don't endanger mother dogs just to meet the increasing demand in our pet-starved country.

A family once came to my store with a frail-looking Shih Tzu puppy to buy products and food. The puppy appeared weak and was visibly struggling with some affliction. When I inquired further, the family told me they had adopted the puppy through OLX. I was dumbfounded—it was the first time I had heard of anyone adopting puppies through OLX. To me, it was just a classifieds site where you would go to find second-hand furniture or old electronic appliances for cheap.

The breeders who sold them the pup were absolute scammers. The poor puppy was crossbred and had multiple hereditary complications, including a severe kidney issue. Shih Tzus are known to be very picky eaters, and with its condition, the puppy was prescribed specific food that the poor soul wouldn't touch. The family was in shambles, but they were doing their best to ensure it had a better life. This is just one of many such incidents I have encountered over the years. It is absolutely necessary to do thorough research before choosing a breeder to adopt a puppy from.

By going to a responsible breeder, you can ensure that you are getting a puppy from someone who focuses on producing healthy dogs with good temperaments. These breeders often invest a lot of time and resources into ensuring the well-being of their dogs, and they can provide detailed information about the puppy's parentage, including any potential health issues that may arise down the line.

A reputable breeder will welcome your questions and will be more than willing to provide health clearances for their dogs. They will take the time to ensure that their puppies go to good homes rather than making a quick sale. They might even ask you questions to make sure you are a good fit for one of their puppies, demonstrating their commitment to the welfare of the animals they breed.

What to Look For

Whether you're at a shelter or visiting a breeder's home, the moment you meet potential furry friends is incredibly exciting and filled with anticipation. The sight of wagging tails and the sound of joyful barks can be heartwarming. However, it's crucial not to let those charming puppy dog eyes cloud your judgment entirely. Here are some important things to carefully observe and consider:

Temperament: Does the dog seem friendly and curious, or do they appear shy and fearful? A dog's behavior during your initial meeting can provide significant clues about their personality and how they might fit into your home.

Energy Level: Is the dog bouncing off the walls with boundless energy, or are they calmly observing their surroundings? This can indicate how much exercise and mental stimulation they will need on a daily basis to remain happy and healthy.

Health: Look for clear, bright eyes, a shiny and well-groomed coat, and no signs of limping or physical distress. Don't hesitate to ask about the dog's medical history, including any past illnesses or ongoing health conditions.

Interaction: Pay attention to how the dog interacts with you, other people, and other dogs. This can provide valuable insight into their socialization skills and potential behavioral issues, which are important factors in ensuring a harmonious household.

Age: Puppies are undeniably adorable but require a significant amount of time, effort, and training. Adult dogs might be calmer and could already be house-trained, making the transition smoother. Senior dogs, on the other hand, can make wonderful, low-key companions who are often already well-adjusted to living with humans.

Taking these observations into account will help you make a well-informed decision, ensuring that your new furry friend is a perfect match for your lifestyle and home environment.

The Breed Factor: More Than Just Looks

While every dog is an individual with its own unique personality and quirks, breed characteristics can give you a general idea of what to expect in terms of temperament, exercise needs, and potential health issues. These breed traits can help guide your decision and manage your expectations when choosing a dog. However, it's important not to get too hung up on breeds –

plenty of mixed-breed dogs make fantastic pets, often with fewer health issues than some purebreds. Mixed-breed dogs can combine the best traits of their different ancestries, offering a unique and rewarding companionship.

That said, if you're drawn to a particular breed, it's crucial to do your research thoroughly. Each breed has its own set of needs and characteristics that might require specific care and attention. For instance, the Australian Shepherd might catch your eye with its beautiful coat and intelligent expression, but are you prepared for its high energy and need for mental stimulation? This breed thrives on having a job to do, and without enough physical and mental activity, an Australian Shepherd can become bored and potentially destructive. On the other hand, the French Bulldog might seem like the perfect apartment dog due to its small size and affectionate nature, but can you handle potential breathing issues and a low tolerance for heat? French Bulldogs are prone to brachycephalic syndrome, which can require special care and attention, especially in warmer climates.

Choosing a dog is a significant commitment that involves considering not only your lifestyle and preferences but also the specific needs and characteristics of the dog. Whether you opt for a purebred or a mixed-breed, the most important thing is to ensure that you are prepared to meet your new pet's needs and provide a loving, stable home.

I have shared a breed matrix later in this chapter which can help you decide which breed suits you best.

The Family Affair

If you have children or other pets, they need to be part of the equation when deciding on a new dog. Some breeds are known for being particularly good with kids, showing patience and gentleness that can be crucial in a family setting. These breeds often enjoy playing and can handle the energy and noise that comes with having children around. On the other hand, some breeds might not have the patience for little hands and loud noises, which can lead to stress for both the dog and your family members.

Similarly, if you have cats or other dogs, you'll want to choose a dog that can coexist peacefully with your current furry family members. Some breeds are known for their ability to get along well with other animals, reducing the risk of conflicts or territorial behavior. Ensuring a harmonious household is essential for the well-being of all your pets, as well as for maintaining a stress-free environment for you and your family.

The Long Haul

Remember, choosing a dog isn't just about finding a companion for the next few months or years – it's a long-term commitment that requires careful consideration. Most dogs live 10-15 years, with some smaller breeds living even longer, sometimes exceeding 20 years. Are you ready for that level of commitment? Can you provide a stable and loving home for that long? It's essential to think long-term when making your decision, considering not just your current lifestyle but also potential changes in the future. This includes your living situation, work schedule, and even your financial stability. Owning a dog means being responsible for their well-being, including regular vet visits, proper nutrition, exercise, and social interaction. It's a rewarding but significant responsibility that should not be taken lightly.

Trust Your Gut (But Use Your Head)

At the end of the day, choosing a dog is a bit like falling in love. Sometimes, you just know when you've found the right one. That inexplicable connection, that feeling of "this is the one," is important. However, unlike in romantic comedies where the heart alone rules the decision, it shouldn't be the only factor you consider when choosing a furry companion.

Consider the story of Manas and his Beagle, Snoopy. Mark fell in love with Snoopy's floppy ears and soulful eyes the moment he saw him at the shelter. But his decision wasn't purely based on emotions. Mark also did his homework, researching the Beagle breed thoroughly. He learned about the breed's tendency to bark, its high energy levels, and its need for regular exercise. He made sure he could provide a home with suitable yard space and neighbors who wouldn't mind the occasional howling. He even looked into the Beagle's dietary needs and potential health issues to ensure he was fully prepared. The result? A match made in doggy heaven, where both owner and pet live in harmony and mutual happiness.

Mark's thoughtful approach ensured that Snoopy's needs are met, and their bond grows stronger every day. This example shows how important it is to balance that initial emotional connection with practical considerations to create a lasting and fulfilling relationship with your pet.

Breed Matrix

The table at the end of the chapter gives an idea about different breeds and their unique characteristics. It compares various aspects of each breed that you should consider. However, it doesn't cover everything you need to consider. While the matrix provides a good overview, it's always better to do more research and gather as much detail as possible, and preferably make a choice which suits your personality as well.

Choosing your perfect canine match is just the beginning of a wonderful journey that will bring immense joy and fulfillment to your life. It's the start of years filled with walks, play, cuddles, and unconditional love that only a dog can offer. It's about finding not just a pet, but a loyal companion, a cherished family member, and a true friend who will stand by your side through thick and thin.

So take your time, do your research, and be honest with yourself about what you can offer a dog and what you're looking for in return. Consider your lifestyle, living situation, and the amount of time and resources you can dedicate to your new furry friend. Whether you end up with a purebred puppy with boundless energy, a senior shelter dog with a heart full of wisdom and love, or anything in between, the perfect match is out there waiting for you. And when you find them, you'll be embarking on one of life's greatest adventures – the journey of companionship with your new best friend. This journey will be filled with countless memories, shared experiences, and a bond that grows stronger with each passing day.

Category	Toy (up to 5 kg)	Small (5-10 kg)	Medium (10-25 kg)	Large (25-40 kg)	Giant (over 40 kg)
Examples	Chihuahua, Yorkshire Terrier, Pomeranian, Toy Poodle, Maltese	Jack Russell Terrier, Miniature Schnauzer, Pug, Shih Tzu, Dachshund	Indian Pariah Dog, Beagle, Border Collie, Bulldog, Cocker Spaniel, Whippet	Labrador Retriever, German Shepherd, Golden Retriever, Boxer, Siberian Husky	Great Dane, Saint Bernard, Newfoundland, Mastiff, Irish Wolfhound
Temperament	Often energetic and alert Can be protective and vocal May be timid around strangers Often form strong bonds with one person	Often confident and spirited Can be stubborn or independent Many have strong prey drives Generally playful and affectionate	Wide range of temperaments Many are working breeds with high intelligence Can be energetic Often loyal and affectionate	Often confident and calm Many are working breeds with strong loyalty Can be protective of family Generally patient and good-natured	Often gentle giants Typically calm and patient Can be protective but not usually aggressive May be prone to laziness

Category	Toy (up to 5 kg)	Small (5-10 kg)	Medium (10-25 kg)	Large (25-40 kg)	Giant (over 40 kg)
Physical needs	Low to moderate exercise needs Short walks and indoor play often sufficient Mental stimulation important	Moderate exercise needs Daily walks and play sessions important Some breeds need mental stimulation	Moderate to high exercise needs Many require daily vigorous exercise Some need jobs or activities	High exercise needs Require space for activity Many need jobs or structured exercise	Moderate exercise needs Short walks and playtime sufficient Prone to joint issues, so exercise should be controlled

Category	Toy (up to 5 kg)	Small (5-10 kg)	Medium (10-25 kg)	Large (25-40 kg)	Giant (over 40 kg)
Friendliness	Often friendly with family May be reserved with strangers Can be good with children if socialized early	Usually good with families Often friendly with strangers May have high energy around children	Generally good with families Socialization important for some breeds Many are good with children	Usually good with families Often friendly but may be aloof with strangers Many excellent with children	Generally excellent with families Often good with children May be intimidating to strangers due to size

Category	Toy (up to 5 kg)	Small (5-10 kg)	Medium (10-25 kg)	Large (25-40 kg)	Giant (over 40 kg)
Trainability	Can be challenging due to stubbornness Positive reinforcement works best	Varies by breed Some highly trainable, others stubborn Consistency and patience important	Often highly trainable Many excel in obedience and agility Some breeds may be independent	Generally highly trainable - Many breeds eager to please Excel in various dog sports and as working dogs	Can be challenging due to size Often respond well to gentle, consistent training May have a stubborn streak

Category	Toy (up to 5 kg)	Small (5-10 kg)	Medium (10-25 kg)	Large (25-40 kg)	Giant (over 40 kg)
Intelligence	Often highly intelligent Quick learners but may be willful Excel in agility and obedience	Generally smart and quick learners Some breeds highly intelligent May outsmart owners at times	Many breeds in this category are highly intelligent Quick learners, especially working breeds Need mental stimulation to prevent boredom	Many breeds highly intelligent Quick learners and problem-solvers Some breeds rank among the smartest dogs	Intelligence varies by breed Many are steady and thoughtful rather than quick Can be independent thinkers

Category	Toy (up to 5 kg)	Small (5-10 kg)	Medium (10-25 kg)	Large (25-40 kg)	Giant (over 40 kg)
Grooming Requirements	Varies by breed Many require regular professional grooming Daily brushing for long-haired breeds	Generally easy to moderate Short-haired breeds need occasional brushing	Varies widely by breed Some require professional grooming Double-coated breeds often shed heavily	Varies by breed Many shed heavily Some require regular professional grooming	Regular brushing needed Many drool extensively Some have high-maintenance coats

Category	Toy (up to 5 kg)	Small (5-10 kg)	Medium (10-25 kg)	Large (25-40 kg)	Giant (over 40 kg)
Common Health Issues	Dental issues Patellar luxation Tracheal collapse Hypoglycemia	Intervertebral disk disease (in long-backed breeds) Brachycephalic issues (in flat-faced breeds) Eye problems Skin allergies	Hip dysplasia Elbow dysplasia Bloat (in deep-chested breeds) Breed-specific issues (e.g., eye problems in Aussies)	Hip and elbow dysplasia Bloat (especially in deep-chested breeds) Arthritis in older age Some breeds prone to certain cancers	Hip and elbow dysplasia Bloat Heart problems Joint issues Shorter lifespans

Category	Toy (up to 5 kg)	Small (5-10 kg)	Medium (10-25 kg)	Large (25-40 kg)	Giant (over 40 kg)
Other Characteristics	Suitable for apartment living Long lifespans (often 12-16 years) May have specific health concerns Can be fragile, requiring gentle handling	Many adapt well to various living situations Some breeds prone to barking Often good for first-time dog owners Some have specific health concerns	Versatile size for various living situations Some have strong herding or hunting instincts May have specific grooming needs Lifespans typically 10-14 years	Need more space and not ideal for small apartments Can be expensive to feed and care for Lifespans typically 10-12 years Many make excellent working and service dogs	Require significant space High food and care costs Shorter lifespans (6-10 years on average) Not suitable for small living spaces

4. Bringing Your New Friend Home

Congratulations! You've finally chosen your perfect canine companion, and now the moment you've been waiting for is here – the big homecoming! This is an exhilarating day, filled with wagging tails, wet noses, and countless surprises. But don't fret. This chapter will help you navigate through the excitement and prepare for almost anything that could come your way. Before you roll out the red carpet (or perhaps a nice, chewy rug), let's make sure everything is in place for your new furry roommate.

Setting Up for Success

Just as you wouldn't bring a newborn home to an empty nursery, your new dog needs a space carefully prepared for their arrival. Ensuring a welcoming environment will help them transition smoothly and feel at home. Here's your comprehensive checklist for creating a dog-friendly haven:

1. **The Essentials**: Make sure to have food and water bowls ready. I recommend ceramic bowls as they

are less prone to water scaling and usually more hygienic than plastic or stainless steel bowls. A collar and leash are necessary for walks and outings, along with ID tags that include your contact information.

Consider choosing the appropriate collar. Many pet parents now prefer harnesses instead of traditional collars, which can put a lot of pressure on a dog's trachea. This is especially tricky for breeds prone to breathing issues. Talk to a veterinary doctor and buy the one that suits your pet.

Don't forget to stock up on nutritious dog food that is appropriate for their age, size, and any specific dietary needs they might have. Look for reputed pet stores near you and they can always recommend the best food for your furball based on their age and breed.

2. **Cozy Quarters**: Provide a comfortable bed or crate where your dog can retreat for some R&R. This will serve as their personal space, offering a sense of security and comfort. Consider adding a soft blanket or cushion to make it even cozier.

Now, let's tackle a topic that often raises eyebrows in the dog-owning world: the use of crates. If you're imagining a tiny cage that restricts your furry friend's freedom, it's time for a perspective shift. When used correctly, a crate can be your puppy's personal sanctuary, not a prison.

Think of a crate as your dog's studio apartment. It's a space that's all their own, a quiet retreat from the hustle and bustle of family life. Dogs are den animals by nature, and many find comfort in small, enclosed spaces. A properly introduced crate can become a safe haven where your pup can relax, sleep, or enjoy some alone time. Indeed, dogs enjoy alone time too. Don't be misled by popular media into thinking they need constant companionship. Like most species, despite their social nature, dogs appreciate some solitude, especially in a cozy, enclosed space.

The key to successful crate training is positive association. Here's a quick guide:

1. *Choose the right size:* Your dog should be able to stand up, turn around, and lie down comfortably.
2. *Make it cozy:* Add soft bedding and some favorite toys.
3. *Introduce gradually:* Let your pup explore the crate at their own pace. Never force them in.
4. *Create positive associations:* Offer treats, meals, or favorite chew toys in the crate.
5. *Build duration slowly:* Start with short periods and gradually increase the time.

Addressing the Controversy

Now, let's address the elephant in the room – or should I say, the crate in the living room. Some people view crates as cruel, likening them to cages in a zoo. But here's where that comparison falls short:

- **Purpose:** Zoo cages are for containment and display. Crates are personal spaces for rest and security.
- **Duration**: Animals in zoos live in their enclosures. Dogs should only be crated for limited periods.
- **Choice**: When properly trained, many dogs choose to enter their crates voluntarily for naps or quiet time.

Max, a rescue Labrador, developed severe anxiety around

crates due to traumatic experiences. His previous family misunderstood his needs, harshly punishing him by locking him in his crate for extended periods. This treatment created a negative association with crates for Max. His new family on the other hand, understood the delicate nature of his fears and approached the situation with extraordinary patience and compassion.

They began by simply leaving the crate in their living room, door wide open, making it a casual part of the home environment. Throughout the day, they would casually toss high-value treats near and eventually into the crate, creating positive associations without any pressure. They never once attempted to coax or persuade Max to enter - letting him set the pace of his journey to comfort.

Their gentle persistence paid off gradually. First, Max would quickly dart in to retrieve treats. Then, he began investigating the crate on his own terms.

After several weeks, something remarkable happened: Max started choosing the crate as his preferred napping spot. "It was an incredible transformation," Mrs. Mehta shared with pride. "What was once a source of fear became his sanctuary. Now, whenever there's a thunderstorm or any loud noises that used to terrify him, that's exactly where he goes to feel safe and secure."

To ensure your crate remains a positive space for your pet:

Do:

- Use the crate for short periods when you can't supervise your puppy
- Make the crate comfortable and inviting
- Offer treats and praise for entering the crate

Don't:

- Use the crate as punishment
- Leave your dog crated for extended periods
- Crate an anxious dog without proper training

As your dog grows and becomes more trustworthy, you may find you need the crate less. Some dogs will continue to use it as their personal space, while others may prefer a dog bed in the corner. Either way, the crate has served its purpose in providing security during the crucial adaptation period.

Remember, a crate is a tool, not a solution for every situation. It's part of a broader approach to creating a safe, comfortable environment for your new furry family member. Used wisely, it can be a valuable aid in housetraining, preventing destructive behaviours, and giving your dog a space to call their own.

3. **Toys**: Invest in a variety of toys for mental stimulation and physical play. Think squeaky toys, chew toys, and puzzle toys that can keep your dog entertained and engaged. Toys are crucial for preventing boredom and promoting healthy chewing habits.
4. **Grooming Gear**: Equip yourself with brushes, nail clippers, and dog-friendly shampoo for keeping your new friend looking and feeling their best. Regular grooming sessions will not only maintain their coat but also strengthen your bond. Remember to consult with your doctor before giving your pet a bath. Puppies are often not given a bath till the first of vaccinations are complete. Till then, wet wipes are your friend.
5. **Clean-Up Crew**: As you embark on your journey with a new

canine companion, be prepared for the occasional indoor accident. Dogs, especially puppies and those adjusting to a new environment, may have mishaps. It's crucial to approach these situations with patience and understanding.

One behavior you might encounter is territorial marking. Dogs often urinate in small amounts on various objects to leave their scent and claim their territory. This instinctive behaviour can be more pronounced in male dogs, particularly those who haven't been neutered. While it's natural for dogs to mark outdoors, indoor marking can become a problem.

To address this issue:

- Establish a consistent potty routine: Regular bathroom breaks help prevent accidents.
- Use positive reinforcement: Reward your dog with treats and praise when they eliminate in the appropriate area.
- Clean thoroughly: Use enzymatic cleaners to completely remove odors, as lingering scents can encourage repeat marking.
- Consider neutering: This can significantly reduce marking behaviour in male dogs.
- Supervise closely: Keep a watchful eye on your dog indoors, especially in new environments.

Remember, correction takes time and consistency. With patience and positive reinforcement, most dogs can be trained to eliminate appropriately.

To handle inevitable accidents, stock up on enzymatic cleaners designed specifically for pet messes. These products break down odor-causing bacteria, discouraging repeat incidents. Don't forget to keep plenty of poop bags on hand for walks to ensure you're always prepared for clean-up duty, both indoors and out.

6. **Puppy Proofing**: Envision your new canine companion as an inquisitive toddler on four paws, ready to explore the world with their mouth as their primary tool of discovery. This natural curiosity, while endearing, necessitates a thorough approach to creating a safe environment.

Here's how to ensure your home is a secure haven for your furry friend:

1. **Electrical Safety**: Secure all loose wires and cords, placing them out of reach or using protective coverings. Exposed wires can be a shocking hazard for a curious pup.
2. **Toxic-Free Zone**: Relocate houseplants to elevated areas or rooms your dog can't access. Many common houseplants, such as lilies and aloe vera, can be toxic if ingested. Research pet-safe alternatives to keep your home both green and dog-friendly.
3. **Chemical Containment**: Store all cleaning supplies, medications, and other potentially harmful substances in securely closed cabinets or high shelves. Remember, a dog's sense of smell is far superior to ours, and they may be attracted to scents we can't even detect.
4. **Choking Hazards**: Survey your home from a dog's eye level. Small objects like coins, buttons, or children's toys can be tempting chew toys that pose serious choking risks. Keep floors clear and teach children to put away their belongings.
5. **Secure Trash**: Invest in a dog-proof trash can with a tight-fitting lid. The kitchen garbage can be an irresistible treasure trove of smells for your new pet, but it's full of potential dangers like chicken bones or spoiled food.

By addressing these concerns, you're not just preventing potential hazards; you're creating a nurturing environment where your new companion can thrive, explore safely, and begin their journey as a cherished member of your family.

The Trip to A New Home

The trip from the shelter or breeder to your home is your

dog's first adventure with you. Make it a good one! If you're driving, secure your dog safely with a crate or doggy seatbelt. For longer trips, plan for potty breaks and bring water.

This journey might be stressful for your new friend. They're leaving everything they've known behind. Speak softly, offer gentle pets if they seem receptive, and maybe even bring a soft blanket with familiar scents from their previous home to ease the transition.

The First 24 Hours

Imagine being dropped into a completely new environment where everything is foreign – that's how your new dog feels. Here's how to make their first day in their forever home a positive experience:

1. **The Grand Tour**: Let your dog explore their new digs at their own pace. Show them where their food, water, and bed are located.
2. **Potty Protocol**: Take your dog to their designated bathroom area immediately upon arrival. Repeat this frequently throughout the day to start establishing a routine.
3. **Slow and Steady**: Keep things calm and quiet. Now is not the time for a welcome home party with all your friends and neighbors.
4. **Family Introductions**: If you have other pets, introduce them slowly and in a controlled manner. Supervision is key!
5. **Routine Beginnings**: Start as you mean to go on. Begin implementing your planned feeding and walking schedule from day one.

Take it from the Tewatia family, who brought home their rescue dog, Max. They had everything ready – bed, toys, food – but forgot one crucial thing: patience. "We expected Max to settle in immediately," Mrs. Tewatia recalls. "But he was nervous and didn't eat for the first day. We learned to give him space and time to adjust at his own pace. By the end of the week, he was part of the family!"

The First Week: Establishing Patterns

The initial week is crucial for setting up routines and helping your dog adjust to their new life. Here's your game plan:

1. **Consistent Schedule**: Stick to regular times for meals, walks, play, and bedtime. Dogs thrive on routine.
2. **Training Foundations**: Start with basic commands and house rules. Keep sessions short and fun.
3. **Bonding Time**: Spend quality one-on-one time with your new friend. This could be quiet cuddle sessions or gentle play.
4. **Health Check**: Schedule a vet visit for a thorough check-up and to discuss vaccinations, diet, and any health concerns.
5. **Gradual Introductions**: Slowly introduce your dog to new experiences, people, and places. Don't overwhelm them with too much, too soon.

Adjusting to a new home takes time. Your dog might exhibit behaviors like clinginess, shyness, or even temporary regression in house training. This is all normal! Be patient, consistent, and loving.

Some dogs adjust quickly, while others may take weeks or even months to fully settle in. The key is to provide a stable, loving environment and let your dog set the pace.

Once the initial excitement wears off, you might face some challenges. Maybe your angel has turned into a shoe-chewing demon, or your quiet pup has found their voice and won't stop barking.

Don't panic! These issues are common and solvable. The key is to address them calmly and consistently. If you're struggling, don't hesitate to seek help from a professional dog trainer or behaviorist.

Building Your Support Network

Speaking of help, now's the time to build your doggy support network. This includes:

- A trusted veterinarian
- A reliable pet sitter or doggy daycare
- Dog-owning friends for playdates and advice

- Local dog trainers or obedience classes
- Online communities on Facebook and Whatsapp which provide support and information to new pet parents

It takes a village to raise a child, and sometimes it takes one to raise a dog too!

In the whirlwind of new dog ownership, don't forget to celebrate the small wins. The first time your dog responds to their name, their first successful potty trip outside, the moment they finally master 'sit' – these are all cause for celebration.

Take lots of pictures, jot down memorable moments, and don't forget to give yourself a pat on the back too. Bringing a new dog home is a big responsibility, and you're doing great!

Every dog is unique. Be flexible, be patient, and most importantly, enjoy this special time. Before you know it, you won't be able to imagine life without your furry friend.

5. Keeping Your Puppy Healthy

Now that you've brought home your new best friend, it's time to ensure they live their best, healthiest life. Just like humans, dogs need regular check-ups, a balanced diet, exercise, and lots of love to thrive. In this chapter, we'll explore the ins and outs of keeping your furry friend in top shape.

Congratulations on welcoming your new canine companion into your home! As you embark on this exciting journey together, it's crucial to prioritize your dog's health and well-being. Just as humans require regular medical check-ups, a nutritious diet, physical activity, and emotional support to flourish, our four-legged friends have similar needs. Dogs thrive when provided with consistent veterinary care, a well-balanced diet tailored to their specific requirements, regular exercise routines, and an abundance of affection from their human family members.

We'll delve deeper into the various aspects of maintaining your furry friend's health. From choosing the right veterinarian and understanding the importance of vaccinations to creating a balanced diet plan and establishing an exercise regimen that suits your dog's breed and energy levels. We'll also discuss the significance of mental stimulation, proper grooming practices, and how to recognize potential health issues early on.

Finding Your Fur-baby's Doctor

First things first: you need a good veterinarian. Think of them as your dog's paediatrician, dentist, and nutritionist all rolled into one. Here's what to look for:

1. Qualifications and experience: Look for a veterinarian with strong qualifications. Consider their years of practice, any specialisations, and continuing education. If you are part of social groups, advice and experience of pet parents should also be a deciding factor.
2. A clean, well-equipped clinic: The facility should be spotless, odor-free, and organized. Look for modern diagnostic equipment like digital X-ray machines, ultrasound devices, and in-house laboratory facilities. The presence of separate waiting areas for dogs and cats can indicate thoughtful care for patient comfort.
3. Good communication skills (they should be able to explain things clearly): A great vet should be able to break down complex medical terms into common language. They should attend to all your concerns (however stupid they might be, if you are a first time pet parent), provide detailed explanations of diagnoses and treatment plans, and offer clear instructions for at-home care.
4. Emergency services or after-hours care: Inquire about the clinic's policy for emergencies outside regular business hours. Some clinics offer 24/7 services, while others may have partnerships with emergency animal hospitals. Knowing your options in advance can be crucial during unexpected situations.

5. A compassionate approach to both pets and their humans: Observe how the vet interacts with animals. They should be gentle, patient, and able to calm anxious pets. Equally important is their ability to empathise with pet owners, offering emotional support during difficult decisions or diagnoses.

Don't be hesitant about exploring options till you find the right vet. Your dog's health is worth it!

Vaccinations: Your Dog's Shield Against Disease

Vaccines are crucial in protecting your dog from potentially life-threatening diseases. The core vaccines for dogs typically include:

1. Rabies
2. Distemper
3. Parvovirus
4. Adenovirus (Canine Hepatitis)

Your vet may recommend additional vaccines based on your dog's lifestyle and risk factors. Keep in mind that puppies need a series of vaccinations, while adult dogs require regular boosters.

A mother's milk provides immunity to puppies only up to 8–10 weeks of age. Therefore, vaccinations should start after six weeks and follow a strict schedule.

A typical vaccination schedule for a puppy looks like the below table.

Age	Date of Vaccination	Vaccination Against Diseases								Date next vaccine due	Vet
		D	H	L	P	A	P	R	C		
6-8 week		+	+	+	+	+	+	+		–	–
10 week									+	—	–
12 week		+	+	+	+	+	+	+		–	–
10 week									+*	–	–

*Booster

Canine, Distemper, Canine Hepatitis, Leptospirosis, Parainfluenza, Adenovirosis, Parvovirosis, Rabies and Coronovirosis

D - Distemper

H - Hepatitis,

L - Leptospirosis

P - Parainfluenza

A - Adenovirosis

P - Parvovirosis

R - Rabies

C – Coronovirosis

Note:

1. To provide the initial protection for a full year, at least 2 vaccinations will be required
2. All dogs should be kept in for a quarantine period (at least one week upto two weeks) following initial vaccinations
3. Regular booster vaccinations are essential
4. Before vaccination a dog should be free from internal and external parasites
5. A small number of pups may fail to respond to vaccina-

tions

6. Occasional hypersensitivity reactions may occur.

Exercise caution when exposing your puppy to the outside world before completing the first round of vaccinations. A puppy weaned from its mother's milk lacks the ability to fight common viruses. Always consult your veterinarian before deciding to take your puppy for its first walk.

Parasites: Tiny creatures who wreck havoc

Fleas, ticks, and worms are more than just pesky nuisances; these minuscule invaders can wreak havoc on your canine companion's health and well-being. These parasites, though small in size, have the potential to cause significant discomfort, transmit diseases, and even lead to severe health complications if left unchecked. To safeguard your furry friend from these microscopic menaces, it's important to implement a consistent preventative care regimen. Regular treatments, administered as per your veterinarian's recommendations, serve as a crucial line of defense against these unwelcome intruders:

1. Flea and tick prevention (topical treatments or oral medications)
2. Heartworm prevention (usually a monthly oral medication)
3. Regular deworming for intestinal parasites

Due to worm transmission through mother's milk and a puppy's eating habits, regular deworming is essential. A typical deworming routine follows this timeline:

1st deworming: at 5 weeks of age

2nd deworming: at 7 weeks of age

Deworming is repeated monthly until the puppy reaches seven months, then every 3–4 months thereafter.

It's crucial to deworm before any vaccinations and mating.

Some of these parasites can affect humans too, so keeping your dog parasite-free protects the whole family!

Exercise

Physical activity is an essential component of your dog's overall well-being, contributing significantly to both their physical fitness and mental acuity. The optimal exercise regimen for your canine companion is not a one-size-fits-all approach; rather, it should be tailored to your dog's unique characteristics. Factors such as breed, age, health condition, and individual energy levels all play crucial roles in determining the ideal amount and type of exercise your furry friend requires.

For instance, high-energy breeds like Border Collies or Australian Shepherds may thrive on several hours of intense physical activity daily, including long runs, challenging fetch sessions, or complex agility courses. These breeds often have a seemingly inexhaustible reservoir of energy and a strong drive to work or play. On the other hand, brachycephalic breeds such as Bulldogs or Pugs, due to their unique facial structure and potential breathing difficulties, might be more suited to shorter, less intense exercise sessions, such as leisurely walks or gentle play in cooler environments.

Regardless of your dog's specific exercise requirements, the key is to make physical activity an enjoyable and engaging experience for both you and your pet. Experiment with a variety of activities to discover what resonates best with your dog's preferences and abilities. Traditional games like fetch or tug-of-war can provide excellent physical workouts while strengthening the bond between you and your furry companion. For dogs who love water, swimming can offer a low-impact, full-body workout that's especially beneficial for older dogs or those with joint issues. More adventurous pet parents might explore organized canine sports such as agility courses, flyball, or even dog parkour, which can provide mental stimulation alongside physical exercise.

The goal is not just to expend energy, but to create positive experiences that enrich your dog's life and deepen your connection.

Mental Health: It's All in Their Head (And That's Important!)

Just as humans can experience a range of mental health issues, our canine companions are also susceptible to emotional and psychological challenges. Dogs can develop stress, anxiety, and even depression, which can manifest in various ways. It's crucial for pet owners to be vigilant and recognize potential signs of mental distress in their furry friends. These indicators may include, but are not limited to, noticeable changes in appetite (either increased or decreased), excessive grooming behaviours such as persistent licking or chewing, alterations in sleep patterns (particularly increased sleeping), and the emergence of destructive behaviors that were previously absent.

To promote and maintain your dog's mental well-being, it's essential to provide a stimulating and enriching environment. Engage your pet's mind with interactive puzzle toys that challenge their problem-solving skills and keep them mentally sharp. Regular training sessions not only reinforce good behaviour but also provide valuable mental stimulation and strengthen the bond between you and your dog.

Introducing your furry companion to new experiences, such as exploring different environments or meeting new (friendly) dogs, can help prevent boredom and reduce anxiety. Perhaps most importantly, never underestimate the profound impact of quality time spent with you – their cherished human companion. Your presence, attention, and affection play a pivotal role in your dog's emotional health and overall happiness.

It's crucial to remember that a puppy's environment significantly affects their personality and behaviour. Domestic conflicts between family members often lead to unwanted behaviours in dogs. Like children, dogs learn about life—including right and wrong—from their caregivers. Just as you would shield a child from negative situations, you must protect your puppy in the same way.

Grooming

Regular grooming is not merely a cosmetic endeavour to keep your canine companion looking dapper (though that's certainly a delightful side effect). It's a crucial component of your dog's overall health care regimen, playing a vital role in maintaining their physical well-being and comfort. The grooming process encompasses a variety of essential practices, each contributing to your furry friend's health in unique ways:

1. **Brushing**: This seemingly simple act serves multiple purposes. It effectively removes dead hair, preventing matting and reducing shedding around your home. More importantly, it helps distribute natural skin oils throughout your dog's coat, promoting a healthy, shiny appearance and maintaining optimal skin condition.
2. **Nail trimming**: Regular nail maintenance is more than just a cosmetic concern. Overgrown nails can cause discomfort and pain for your dog, potentially leading to altered gait patterns and even skeletal issues over time. Proper nail care prevents these problems and reduces the risk of accidental injuries from snagged or split nails.
3. **Dental hygiene**: Just like humans, dogs require regular oral care. Routine teeth cleaning helps prevent the build-up of plaque and tartar, reducing the risk of periodontal disease. This not only maintains fresh breath but also protects against more serious health issues that can stem from poor dental hygiene, such as heart and kidney problems.
4. **Health check**: Grooming sessions provide an excellent opportunity for a hands-on health inspection. As you

brush, bathe, or trim your dog, you can carefully examine their skin and body for any unusual lumps, bumps, or changes in texture. This proactive approach allows for early detection of potential health issues, from skin conditions to more serious concerns like fleas/ticks or tumours.

Beyond these health benefits, regular grooming sessions foster a strong bond between you and your canine companion. These moments of focused attention and gentle touch can be incredibly soothing for your dog, reducing stress and anxiety while strengthening your emotional connection. It's an opportunity to show your pet love and care in a tangible way, reinforcing your role as their trusted caregiver and friend.

Recognizing Health Red Flags

While regular veterinary check-ups are essential for maintaining your dog's health, as a responsible pet owner, you play a crucial role in monitoring your furry friend's well-being on a daily basis. Your attentiveness and quick action can make a significant difference in detecting potential health issues early. Be vigilant and observe your dog closely for any of the following signs that may indicate a health concern:

1. Changes in appetite or water consumption: A sudden increase or decrease in food or water intake can be a sign of various health issues, including dental problems, digestive disorders, or hormonal imbalances.
2. Unusual lethargy or changes in behavior: If your typically energetic dog becomes unusually lethargic or displays significant changes in behaviour, such as increased aggression or withdrawal, it could indicate underlying health problems or pain.

3. Gastrointestinal disturbances: Persistent vomiting or diarrhoea can lead to dehydration and may be symptoms of various conditions, from dietary indiscretion to more serious illnesses.
4. Respiratory issues: Coughing, sneezing, or difficulty breathing could be signs of respiratory infections, allergies, or heart problems. Pay attention to any changes in your dog's breathing patterns or unusual sounds.
5. Mobility problems: Limping, difficulty moving, or reluctance to engage in usual physical activities might indicate joint issues, injuries, or neurological problems.

6. Changes in urination habits: Increased frequency, difficulty urinating, or changes in urine color or odor could

signal urinary tract infections, kidney problems, or other health issues.

7. Skin and coat changes: Excessive scratching, hair loss, or changes in skin appearance may indicate allergies, parasites, or hormonal imbalances.
8. Eye and ear abnormalities: Redness, discharge, or excessive scratching around the eyes or ears could be signs of infections or allergies.

You know your dog best, and any persistent or concerning changes in their appearance, behaviour, or bodily functions warrant attention. When in doubt, it's always prudent to consult with your veterinarian. Early detection and intervention can often lead to more favourable outcomes and potentially simpler, less invasive treatments. A proactive approach to your dog's health is an integral part of providing them with the best possible care and ensuring a long, happy life together.

Caring for your dog's health might seem like a big responsibility – and it is! But it's also one of the most rewarding aspects of dog ownership. Every belly rub, every wagging tail, every excited bark when you come home – these are the dividends of your investment in your dog's health and happiness.

And you're not alone on this journey. Your veterinarian, fellow dog owners, and a wealth of reputable online resources are all there to support you. And at the end of the day, no one knows your dog better than you do. Trust your instincts, shower them with love, and enjoy every moment of your life together.

6. Puppy Nutrition

Just as a high-performance car needs the right fuel to run smoothly, your dog needs the right nutrition to stay healthy, active, and happy. But with countless options lining pet store shelves and passionate debates about raw diets, grain-free options, and homemade meals, how do you navigate the world of canine cuisine? Buckle up, because we're about to embark on a journey through the tasty (and sometimes confusing) world of dog nutrition!

The Basics: What Does Your Dog Really Need?

At its core, a dog's diet needs to provide:

1. Proteins: For muscle development and repair
2. Fats: For energy and a healthy coat
3. Carbohydrates: For energy and digestive health
4. Vitamins and minerals: For various bodily functions
5. Water: The often-overlooked but crucial component of any diet

The exact balance of these nutrients can vary based on your dog's age, size, breed, and activity level. A working Border Collie will have different nutritional needs than a senior Chihuahua lounging on the couch!

What to feed your dog

With the myriad of options available in pet stores, online retailers, and specialty shops, selecting the ideal food for your canine companion can be a daunting task. The sheer variety of brands, formulations, and ingredient lists can leave even the most dedicated pet parent feeling overwhelmed and uncertain. From grain-free options to raw diets, from breed-specific formulas to age-targeted meals, the choices seem endless. Moreover, conflicting information from various sources – be it online forums, well-meaning friends, or marketing claims – can further complicate the decision-making process. However, you can navigate this nutritional maze to find the perfect diet that will keep your furry friend healthy, happy, and thriving.

These guidelines below will help you decide:

1. Choose foods that adhere to official nutritional standards (such as IS 11968 : 2019), ensuring your dog receives

a balanced and complete diet that meets regulatory requirements.

2. Tailor your dog's diet to their specific life stage, body size, and activity level, as nutritional needs can vary significantly throughout a dog's life and between different breeds.
3. Be vigilant about any food sensitivities or allergies your dog may have, and adjust their diet accordingly to avoid potential health issues or discomfort.
4. Seek professional guidance from your veterinarian regarding your dog's nutritional needs, as they can provide personalized recommendations based on your pet's individual health status, breed characteristics, and lifestyle factors.
5. Consider the quality of ingredients in your chosen dog food, opting for products with whole, identifiable protein sources and avoiding those with excessive fillers or artificial additives

Growing puppies need a diet rich in protein, fat, carbohydrates, minerals, and vitamins for proper bone and tissue development. While dogs are naturally carnivores—their most natural diet consisting of raw meat, bones, and occasional greens—we must be cautious about raw meat due to the risk of worms and infections.

Boiled meat is preferable to raw. Oatmeal and cornmeal, when boiled, make excellent food. Bones with a small amount of meat attached can be boiled along with either meal for a nutritious meal.

Feeding schedule:

1. Weaning to 3 months

Due to developing digestive organs, puppies require smaller, more frequent meals. Feed 4–5 times a day, with a total quantity of 150–500 grams per day (depending on breed).

8 AM: Half-boiled eggs, 100–200 ml milk, cereal biscuits, egg Cerelac, or cornflakes
12 PM: Curd, rice, pulses, and green vegetables
5 PM: Same as noon
9 PM: Same as morning

2. 3 to 6 months

As the dog grows, the quantity should be increased and frequency decreased. Only three meals a day are required, with a total quantity of 300–800 grams per day.

8 AM: Egg or milk + dalia, Cerelac
1 PM: Curd, juice, soup, rice, cheese, or paneer
6 PM: Minced meat + dalia or rice, liver

3. 6 month onwards

Two meals a day are sufficient; daily quantity should be about 500–1500 grams.
8 AM: Milk + chapati / toasted bread / dalia / boiled vegetables
6 PM: Meat / egg + dalia / rice

As your puppy matures into a full-grown dog, developing their unique personality and individual traits, you'll gain valuable insights into their specific nutritional needs and preferences. This transition period offers an excellent opportunity to gradually introduce a wider variety of foods, tailoring their diet to better suit their evolving requirements. Pay close attention to how your dog responds to different ingredients and textures, noting any particular favorites or potential sensitivities. This process of dietary exploration and adaptation allows you to create a customized feeding plan that not only meets your dog's nutritional needs but also caters to their personal tastes, ensuring both their health and enjoyment at mealtime.

Types of Commercial Dog Food

1. Dry Food (Kibble): This type of dog food is highly convenient for pet owners and offers several benefits. Its crunchy texture can help maintain dental health by reducing plaque buildup. Dry food also has an extended shelf life, making it an economical choice for many dog owners. Additionally, it's easy to store and measure for portion control.
2. Wet Food: Canned or pouched wet food is often more appealing to dogs due to its rich aroma and taste. It has a higher moisture content, which can be beneficial for dogs that don't drink enough water or have certain health conditions. While typically more expensive than dry food, wet food can be a good option for picky eaters or dogs with dental issues.
3. Semi-Moist Food: This type of dog food offers a balance between dry and wet food in terms of texture and moisture content. It's convenient to serve and often comes in

single-serving packages. However, it's important to note that semi-moist food often contains higher levels of sugar and preservatives to maintain its texture and shelf life, which may not be ideal for all dogs.

4. Freeze-Dried/Dehydrated Food: These foods undergo minimal processing, which helps preserve nutrients and natural flavors. They often consist of raw ingredients that have had the moisture removed. While they require some preparation before serving (usually by adding water), they can be a good option for pet owners looking for a more natural diet for their dogs. However, they tend to be more expensive than traditional commercial dog foods.

Supplements

A growing puppy requires a carefully balanced nutritional regimen to support their rapid development. In addition to a well-formulated diet, veterinarians often recommend supplementing with multi-vitamin drops to ensure all essential nutrients are provided. Liver tonic can be beneficial for supporting healthy liver function and overall growth, while calcium tonic is crucial for proper bone and teeth development. It's important to note that these supplements should be administered regularly and in appropriate doses as prescribed by your veterinarian, taking into account your puppy's specific needs, breed, and growth rate. Always consult with your vet before introducing any new supplements to your puppy's diet to ensure they are necessary and safe particularly for your pet.

The most expensive food isn't always the best, and what works for one dog might not work for another.

Tackling Controversial Topics

Grain-Free:

Grain-free diets experienced a surge in popularity among dog owners, driven by marketing claims of improved health benefits. However, recent scientific studies have raised significant concerns about a potential link between these diets and an increased risk of heart problems in certain dog breeds.

This unexpected correlation has prompted veterinarians and pet nutritionists to reassess the widespread adoption of grain-free dog foods. The current consensus among experts is that, for the vast majority of dogs, grains are not only safe but can be a valuable part of a balanced diet. They provide essential nutrients, fiber, and energy.

The takeaway from this evolving understanding is clear: unless your dog has been diagnosed with a specific grain allergy by a veterinarian (which is, in fact, quite rare), there's typically no compelling reason to eliminate grains from their diet. In fact, doing so without proper cause might inadvertently deprive your furry friend of important nutritional benefits.

Raw Diets:

Advocates of raw diets argue that they offer numerous benefits for canine health, including improved coat condition, enhanced dental hygiene, and optimized digestive function. The theory behind raw feeding is rooted in the idea of mimicking a dog's ancestral diet, which primarily consisted of uncooked meats, bones, and occasional plant matter. Proponents claim that this approach can lead to increased energy levels, better weight management, and a stronger immune system.

However, it's crucial to approach raw diets with caution and a thorough understanding of the potential risks involved. One of the primary concerns is the risk of bacterial contamination, particularly from pathogens like Salmonella and E. coli, which can be present in raw meats. These bacteria can not only affect the dog but also pose a risk to human family members through handling of the food or contact with the dog's feces.

Additionally, ensuring nutritional balance in a raw diet can be challenging. Without careful planning and potentially professional guidance, dogs may miss out on essential nutrients, vitamins, or minerals crucial for their overall health and well-being. This is particularly important for growing puppies, pregnant or nursing dogs, and seniors, who have specific nutritional requirements.

Given these considerations, it's imperative to consult with a veterinarian or a canine nutritionist before transitioning to a raw diet. These professionals can provide personalized advice, help create a balanced meal plan, and monitor your dog's health throughout the transition. They can also guide you on safe food handling practices to minimize the risk of bacterial contamination.

If you're interested in the potential benefits of a raw diet but concerned about the risks, there are alternative options to explore. Some pet food companies offer freeze-dried or gently cooked versions of raw diets, which may provide similar benefits with reduced risk of bacterial contamination. These options can serve as a middle ground for pet owners looking to incorporate elements of a raw diet into their dog's nutrition plan.

Homemade Diets:

Preparing homemade meals for your dog can offer greater control over ingredients and quality, but it's essential to ensure the diet is nutritionally balanced and complete. Creating a well-rounded homemade diet requires careful planning and expertise. It's highly recommended to collaborate with a veterinary nutritionist who can help develop a customized recipe tailored to your dog's specific needs.

These professionals have the knowledge and experience to formulate a diet that includes the right balance of proteins, carbohydrates, fats, vitamins, and minerals essential for your dog's optimal health. They can also guide you on proper portion sizes, cooking methods, and any necessary supplements to fill nutritional gaps. While homemade diets can be beneficial, it's crucial to approach them with caution and professional guidance to avoid potential nutritional deficiencies that could impact your dog's long-term health and well-being.

One Size Doesn't Fit All

Puppies:

Puppies need more calories and nutrients to support their rapid growth. Look for foods specifically formulated for puppies, and feed them more frequently than adult dogs.

Senior Dogs:

As dogs enter their golden years, their metabolism slows and their nutritional needs change. Senior dog foods often have fewer calories and may include supplements for joint health.

Weight Management:

Unfortunately, canine obesity is a growing problem.

If your pooch is packing on the kilos, consult your vet about a weight management plan. This might include a special diet and increased exercise.

Treats: The Spice of Life

Treats play a crucial role in training and strengthening the bond between you and your canine companion. However, it's essential to exercise caution, as excessive treat consumption can lead to unwanted weight gain and potential health issues. To maintain a healthy balance, adhere to the widely recommended 10% rule: ensure that treats constitute no more than 10% of your dog's total daily caloric intake. This guideline helps prevent overfeeding while still allowing for the use of treats as positive reinforcement.

When selecting treats, opt for healthy, low-calorie options that align with your dog's dietary needs. Consider alternatives such as small pieces of cooked lean meats, fresh vegetables like carrots or green beans, or specially formulated low-calorie dog treats. These choices can satisfy your dog's cravings without compromising their overall nutrition.

It's important to remember that treats aren't the only way to reward your furry friend. Many dogs find immense joy and satisfaction in non-food rewards. Enthusiastic praise, extra playtime, a favorite toy, or even a quick cuddle session can be just as effective in reinforcing good behavior and strengthening your bond. By diversifying your reward system, you can keep your dog motivated and engaged while maintaining their optimal health and weight.

Feeding Practices: It's Not Just What, But How

Feeding Schedule: Routine is Key

Establishing a consistent feeding schedule is crucial for adult dogs and puppies alike. Most adult dogs thrive on a twice-daily feeding routine, typically with meals in the morning and evening. This schedule aligns well with their natural digestive rhythms and helps maintain stable energy levels throughout the day. Puppies, on the other hand, have higher energy requirements and smaller stomachs, necessitating more frequent feedings. Depending on their age and breed, puppies may need three to four meals spread evenly throughout the day to support their rapid growth and development.

Adhering to a regular feeding schedule offers numerous benefits beyond just satisfying hunger. It aids in digestion by allowing the dog's body to anticipate and prepare for meals, which can lead to more efficient nutrient absorption. A consistent routine also plays a crucial role in house training, especially for puppies, as it helps regulate their bathroom habits. By feeding at set times, you can better predict when your dog will need to eliminate, making it easier to establish a successful potty training regimen.

Moreover, a structured feeding schedule can contribute to better behavior management. Dogs thrive on routine, and knowing when to expect their meals can reduce anxiety and food-related behaviors such as begging or resource guarding. It also provides an opportunity for bonding, as meal times become a predictable and enjoyable part of your dog's day. Remember to be flexible when necessary, such as adjusting meal times to accommodate changes in your dog's activity level or health needs, always in consultation with your veterinarian.

Portion Control: Measuring Matters

Utilize the feeding guidelines provided on your dog food packaging as an initial reference point, but it's crucial to understand that these are merely general recommendations. The ideal portion size for your canine companion can vary significantly based on several individual factors. Your dog's unique metabolism plays a key role in determining their nutritional needs, as some dogs naturally burn calories more quickly than others. Additionally, your pet's activity level is a critical consideration - a highly active dog engaged in regular exercise or work will require more calories than a less active one.

Any existing health conditions may affect their dietary needs. It's also worth noting that the quality and caloric density of the food itself can impact portion sizes. Higher quality, nutrient-dense foods may require smaller portions to meet your dog's nutritional needs compared to lower quality options.

To determine the optimal portion size for your dog, start with the recommended amount and closely monitor your pet's weight and body condition over time. Adjust the portions accordingly if you notice any unwanted weight gain or loss. Regular weigh-ins and body condition assessments can help you fine-tune your dog's diet to maintain their ideal weight and overall health. When in doubt, always consult with your veterinarian for personalized advice on your dog's specific nutritional requirements.

Food Puzzles and Slow Feeders: Making Mealtime Stimulating

For dogs that consume their meals rapidly or require additional mental stimulation, incorporating food puzzles and slow feeders can significantly enhance the dining experience. These innovative feeding tools serve multiple purposes: they encourage slower eating habits, which can aid digestion and prevent issues like bloat, while also providing much-needed mental engagement.

By transforming mealtime into a problem-solving activity, these devices tap into a dog's natural foraging instincts, offering both physical and mental benefits. Slow feeders, which often feature intricate designs or mazes, force dogs to work for their food, effectively slowing down their eating pace. Food puzzles, on the other hand, challenge dogs to figure out how to access their meal, stimulating their minds and keeping them occupied for longer periods.

This approach not only makes feeding time more interesting but can also help alleviate boredom-related behaviors in dogs that finish their meals too quickly. Additionally, the increased time and effort required to eat can contribute to a greater sense of satisfaction and fullness, potentially aiding in weight management for some dogs.

What Not to Feed A Dog

While it's important to know what to feed your dog, it's equally crucial to be aware of foods that can be harmful or even toxic to them. Here's a list of items you should never offer your canine companion:

- **Chocolate:** Contains theobromine, which is toxic to dogs and can cause vomiting, diarrhea, and in severe cases, heart problems and seizures.
- **Xylitol:** This artificial sweetener found in many sugar-free products can cause a rapid drop in blood sugar

and liver failure in dogs.

- **Grapes and raisins:** Can lead to kidney failure in dogs, even in small amounts.
- **Onions and garlic:** These can damage a dog's red blood cells, potentially leading to anemia.
- **Avocados:** Contain persin, which can cause vomiting and diarrhea in dogs.
- **Macadamia nuts:** Can cause weakness, depression, vomiting, and hyperthermia in dogs.
- **Alcohol:** Even small amounts can cause intoxication, leading to vomiting, disorientation, and in severe cases, coma or death.

- **Caffeine:** Found in coffee, tea, and some sodas, it can be fatal to dogs if consumed in large quantities.
- **Raw or undercooked meat, eggs, and bones:** Can con-

tain bacteria that cause food poisoning. Raw eggs also contain an enzyme that can lead to skin and coat problems.

- **Salt:** Large amounts can cause excessive thirst and urination and, in severe cases, sodium ion poisoning.
- **Yeast dough:** Can continue to rise in a dog's stomach, potentially causing gas to accumulate and leading to dangerous bloat.

Note that this list is not exhaustive. If you're ever unsure about whether a food is safe for your dog, it's best to err on the side of caution and consult with your veterinarian. Always keep these harmful foods out of your dog's reach and educate family members and guests about what not to feed your furry friend.

When to See the Vet: Nutritional Red Flags

Watch out for these signs that might indicate a dietary issue:

1. Sudden changes in appetite or water consumption
2. Unexplained weight loss or gain
3. Chronic diarrhea or constipation
4. Dull, dry coat
5. Lethargy or lack of energy

While dog nutrition may seem complex, the basics are simple: provide a balanced diet appropriate for your dog's life stage, keep an eye on portion sizes, and don't forget that love is the most important ingredient of all. Your dog's wagging tail and bright eyes at mealtime are the best indicators that you're doing something right. Here's to many years of happy, healthy eating for your furry friend!

7. Early Training And Socialization

Picture a scenario where your furry companion responds promptly to your call, greets visitors politely without jumping, and confidently navigates the bustle of a dog park. It might sound like an unattainable ideal, but rest assured, this vision can become a tangible reality with the right blend of patience, unwavering consistency, and a well-informed approach to training.

In this fascinating world of dog training, you'll learn to communicate effectively with your four-legged friend, understand their unique needs and instincts, and guide them towards becoming the well-mannered companion you've always envisioned. From mastering basic obedience commands to addressing complex behavioural issues, the path to a harmonious relationship with your dog is paved with rewarding challenges and heartwarming breakthroughs.

The Foundations: Understanding Canine Psychology

Before we dive into specific training techniques, it's crucial to understand how your dog thinks. Dogs aren't tiny humans in fur coats; they have their own unique way of perceiving and interacting with the world.

Speaking Dog: Understanding Canine Communication

As a responsible pet parent, it's crucial to recognize that effective dog training begins with self-preparation. Before embarking on the journey of training your canine companion, you must first cultivate your own skills of observation and mindfulness.

By honing these abilities, you'll gain invaluable insights into your dog's unique behaviours, patterns, and activities. This heightened awareness serves as a foundation for understanding your furry friend on a deeper level, enabling you to tailor your training approach to their individual needs and personality traits.

Moreover, this attentiveness to your dog's subtle cues and responses will significantly enhance your ability to communicate effectively, fostering a stronger bond and facilitating more successful training outcomes. Remember, the process of becoming a skilled dog trainer is a two-way street – as you guide your dog, you'll find yourself growing and learning alongside them, creating a mutually rewarding experience that strengthens your relationship and leads to more harmonious coexistence.

Dogs possess a rich and nuanced communication system that encompasses body language, vocalizations, and scent cues. Mastering the art of interpreting your canine companion's signals is akin to acquiring proficiency in a new language – it demands dedication, patience, and keen observation, but the rewards are truly extraordinary. By developing this skill, you'll gain invaluable insights into your dog's emotional state, needs, and intentions, fostering a deeper connection and more harmonious relationship. To become fluent in "dog language," pay close attention to these key elements:

1. Tail position and movement: The tail serves as a vital communicative tool, with its position, speed, and pattern of movement conveying a wealth of information about your dog's emotional state and intentions.
2. Ear position: The subtle shifts in ear positioning can reveal much about your dog's level of alertness, confidence, or anxiety in any given situation.
3. Eye contact (or lack thereof): The intensity, duration, and nature of eye contact your dog makes – or deliberately avoids – can provide crucial clues about their comfort level and emotional state.
4. Body posture: The overall stance, muscle tension, and

positioning of your dog's body offer a comprehensive picture of their emotional and physical state.

5. Vocalizations: The diverse range of sounds dogs produce, including various types of barks, whines, growls, and even sighs, each carry specific meanings and emotional undertones.
6. Scent marking: While less obvious to human observers, dogs communicate extensively through scent, using urine marking, anal gland secretions, and even paw pad pheromones to convey information to other canines.

By improving your ability to recognize and interpret these multifaceted communication cues, you'll be better equipped to respond appropriately to your dog's needs, emotions, and desires. This enhanced understanding will not only strengthen your bond but also enable you to create a more supportive and enriching environment for your furry friend, ultimately leading to a more fulfilling relationship for both of you.

Positive Reinforcement: The Golden Ticket of Dog Training

Positive reinforcement stands as the fundamental pillar of contemporary dog training methodologies. This approach is elegantly straightforward yet profoundly effective: by rewarding behaviours you wish to encourage, you increase the likelihood of their recurrence. The beauty of positive reinforcement lies in its versatility and the wide array of rewards that can be employed to reinforce desired behaviours. These rewards can encompass a diverse range of incentives, each tailored to your dog's individual preferences and motivations:

1. Treats: From small, low-calorie training treats to pieces of

your dog's regular kibble, or even special high-value treats for particularly challenging tasks.

2. Verbal praise and affection: Enthusiastic words of encouragement, coupled with gentle petting or scratching in your dog's favourite spots (behind the ear, under the chin, the snout, belly rubs, etc.)
3. Toys and playtime: Engaging in a quick game of tug-of-war, offering a favourite chew toy, or tossing a ball for a brief fetch session.
4. Life rewards: Incorporating everyday activities your dog enjoys, such as going for a walk, receiving their meals, or being allowed to greet visitors.
5. Environmental enrichment: Providing opportunities for exploration, sniffing, or access to a preferred resting spot.

It's crucial to emphasize that the timing of the reward is paramount in positive reinforcement training. The reward must be delivered promptly following the desired behaviour to establish a clear and strong association in your dog's mind. This ensures that your canine companion accurately connects the reward with the specific action you're aiming to reinforce, thereby increasing the likelihood of the behaviour being repeated in the future.

As you progress in your training journey, you'll discover that consistency in both timing and the type of rewards used will significantly enhance the effectiveness of your positive reinforcement efforts, leading to more reliable and lasting results in your dog's behaviour.

Basic Obedience: The Building Blocks of Good Behaviour

Every well-trained and well-mannered canine companion should have a solid foundation in these essential obedience commands, which form the cornerstone of effective communication between you and your furry friend:

1. Sit: A fundamental command that teaches your dog to remain in a seated position, promoting calmness and focus.
2. Stay: This crucial command instructs your dog to maintain their current position until released, enhancing their impulse control and safety.
3. Come: Also known as "recall," this command is vital for your dog's safety and ensures they return to you promptly when called.
4. Down: Teaching your dog to lie down on command can help manage their energy levels and is useful in various situations.
5. Leave it: This important command helps prevent your dog from interacting with potentially dangerous or inappropriate items.

Let's delve deeper into the process of teaching the "Come" command, which is widely regarded as one of the most critical commands for ensuring your dog's safety and well-being:

1. Begin your training sessions in an environment with minimal distractions, allowing your dog to focus solely on you and the task at hand.
2. Capture your dog's attention by enthusiastically calling their name, followed by a clear and upbeat "Come!" command. Your tone should convey excitement and positivity.
3. The moment your dog responds and approaches you, shower them with effusive praise and immediately offer a high-value treat as a reward. This positive reinforcement strengthens the association between the command and the desired behaviour.

4. As your dog becomes more proficient, gradually introduce greater challenges by increasing the distance between you and your pet, as well as incorporating more distracting elements into the training environment.

It's crucial to remember that the "Come" command should invariably be associated with positive experiences for your dog. Under no circumstances should you use this command to summon your dog for punishment or any unpleasant activity. Doing so could undermine their trust and willingness to respond to the command in the future.

Training Tools: Clickers, Whistles, and More

While verbal commands and hand signals are the most common methods of communication in dog training, various devices can enhance your training sessions and provide clearer, more consistent cues to your canine companion. Let's explore some popular training tools:

Clicker Training

Clicker training is a highly effective and widely adopted method in dog training that utilizes a small, handheld device capable of producing a distinctive clicking sound. This innovative approach harnesses the power of precise timing and consistent auditory cues to reinforce desired behaviours in your canine companion. Let's delve into the intricacies of how clicker training operates:

1. The click sound serves as a precise marker, pinpointing the exact moment your dog exhibits the desired behaviour. This instantaneous feedback helps your dog understand precisely which action is being rewarded.

2. Immediately following the click, you provide your dog with a tangible reward, such as a treat, or offer enthusiastic praise. This swift reinforcement strengthens the association between the desired behaviour and the positive outcome.
3. Through consistent repetition, your dog begins to form a strong mental connection between the click sound and the ensuing positive reinforcement. This association transforms the clicker into a powerful and versatile training tool, capable of shaping a wide range of behaviours.
4. As your dog becomes more attuned to the clicker, you can use it to capture and reinforce increasingly complex behaviours, allowing for the development of intricate tricks and commands.

Clickers excel in their ability to provide incredibly precise timing, making them invaluable for shaping nuanced behaviours and fine-tuning your dog's responses. This precision allows trainers to communicate exactly which aspect of a behaviour is correct, facilitating rapid learning and the acquisition of complex skills. Moreover, the consistent and neutral nature of the click sound helps eliminate confusion that may arise from variations in verbal praise or inconsistent timing, thereby accelerating the learning process and enhancing the overall effectiveness of your training sessions.

Whistle Training

Whistle training is a highly effective method for outdoor training scenarios and situations where dogs need to be commanded from a distance. This versatile tool offers several key advantages:

1. Produces a consistent and distinctive sound that can be heard over considerable distances, making it ideal for large open spaces
2. Particularly beneficial for working dogs, such as hunting or herding breeds, that often operate at a distance from their handlers
3. Proves invaluable in noisy or distracting environments where verbal commands might be difficult to hear
4. Can be utilized to teach and reinforce a wide range of commands, from basic recall to more complex behaviours
5. Offers a clear, uniform cue that remains consistent regardless of the handler's emotional state or voice variations

To begin whistle training, it's essential to create a positive association between the whistle sound and rewards. This foundation can be established through the following steps:

1. Introduce the whistle sound in a calm, distraction-free environment
2. Immediately follow each whistle blast with a high-value treat or reward
3. Repeat this process frequently to strengthen the positive association

Once your dog consistently responds positively to the whistle, you can gradually introduce specific commands using different whistle patterns. For example:

1. One short blast for "sit"
2. Two short blasts for "come"
3. One long blast for "stay"

Remember to be patient and consistent in your training approach, always reinforcing desired behaviours with rewards. With time and practice, your dog will learn to respond reliably to whistle commands, enhancing your ability to communicate effectively over long distances or in challenging environments.

Remote Training Collars

Remote training collars are electronic devices capable of delivering various stimuli such as auditory cues, vibrations, or mild static corrections. While their use remains a topic of debate within the dog training community, proponents argue that when employed judiciously and humanely under expert guidance, these tools can yield positive results in specific training scenarios. Some potential applications include:

1. Facilitating off-leash training in controlled environments, allowing for greater freedom of movement while maintaining reliable recall

2. Addressing persistent behavioural challenges that have proven resistant to traditional training methods
3. Assisting in the training of hearing-impaired dogs by providing alternative sensory cues
4. Reinforcing boundaries and safety protocols in potentially hazardous situations

It is imperative to emphasize that the use of remote training collars requires careful consideration and should only be undertaken under the close supervision of a certified professional trainer. This ensures that the device is used appropriately, minimizing any potential for misuse or unintended negative consequences. Proper training in the collar's operation and a thorough understanding of canine behaviour and learning principles are essential prerequisites for its effective and ethical application.

Target Sticks

A target stick is an innovative training tool consisting of a long, slender pole designed to guide and direct your dog's movements with precision. This versatile instrument serves multiple purposes in canine training and behaviour modification:

1. Teaching precise positions or movements: The target stick allows you to shape specific behaviours by encouraging your dog to follow the stick's tip, enabling you to guide them into desired positions or through complex sequences of movements.
2. Helping shy or anxious dogs build confidence: By providing a focal point and encouraging interaction, the target stick can help timid dogs gradually become more comfortable with new experiences and environments.
3. Facilitating the training of intricate tricks and behaviours: The stick's ability to provide clear, visual cues makes it an

excellent aid for teaching advanced tricks or refining existing behaviours to a higher level of precision.

4. Enhancing communication between handler and dog: As a non-verbal cue, the target stick can improve the clarity and consistency of your training signals, reducing confusion and accelerating the learning process.

To begin incorporating a target stick into your training regimen, start by teaching your dog to touch the end of the stick with their nose. This foundational behaviour, often referred to as "targeting," can then be expanded upon to create more complex behaviours and routines. As your dog becomes proficient with the basic targeting behaviour, you can gradually increase the difficulty by introducing movement, distance, and duration to the exercises.

Remember, while these tools can be valuable aids in training, they are not substitutes for patience, consistency, and positive reinforcement. Always prioritize building a strong, trust-based relationship with your dog throughout the training process.

Socialization: Creating a Confident Canine

Proper socialization is a cornerstone of raising a well-adjusted and confident canine companion. While the critical socialization period typically occurs between 3 and 16 weeks of age, it's important to note that socialization efforts can and should continue throughout a dog's life. During this formative period, puppies are particularly receptive to new experiences, making it an ideal time to lay the foundation for positive associations with various stimuli. However, even if you've adopted an older dog or missed this early window, don't be discouraged – socialization can still yield significant benefits at any age with patience and consistency.

To ensure comprehensive socialization, aim to expose your dog to a diverse array of experiences, including:

1. People: Introduce your dog to individuals of different ages, races, genders, and physical appearances. This includes people wearing hats, sunglasses, or uniforms, as well as those using mobility aids like wheelchairs or crutches.
2. Animals: Facilitate positive interactions with various species, including other dogs of different breeds and sizes, cats, and even farm animals if possible. Ensure these encounters are carefully supervised to maintain safety.
3. Environments: Familiarize your dog with a wide range of settings, such as urban areas, parks, beaches, forests, and different types of flooring (e.g., grass, concrete, carpet). This environmental exposure helps build adaptability and confidence.
4. Sounds: Gradually introduce your dog to diverse auditory stimuli, including household appliances, traffic noise, thunderstorms, and fireworks. Use recordings or apps designed for dog socialization to control the volume and duration of exposure.
5. Objects: Allow your dog to investigate various objects like umbrellas, balloons, bicycles, and household items. This exploration helps prevent fear responses to unfamiliar items in the future.

When conducting socialization exercises, it's paramount to ensure that each experience is positive and rewarding for your dog. Use treats, praise, and play to create pleasant associations with new stimuli. Never force your dog into uncomfortable situations, as this can lead to negative associations and potentially exacerbate fear or anxiety. Instead, allow your dog to approach new experiences at their own pace, always providing an "escape route" if they feel overwhelmed.

Socialization is an ongoing process. Even after the critical period, continue to expose your dog to new experiences in a controlled and positive manner. This lifelong approach to socialization helps maintain your dog's confidence and adaptability, fostering a well-rounded and sociable canine companion.

Problem Behaviours: Nipping Issues in the Bud

Even the most well-behaved dogs can occasionally exhibit problematic behaviours. It's essential to address these issues promptly and effectively to maintain a harmonious relationship with your canine companion. Here's a comprehensive guide on how to tackle some of the most common behavioural challenges:

Jumping Up

Jumping up is a natural greeting behaviour for dogs, but it can be problematic, especially with larger breeds or when interacting with children or elderly individuals. To curb this behaviour:

1. Consistently ignore the jumping behaviour. This means no eye contact, no speaking, and no physical interaction when your dog jumps.
2. Reward your dog with attention, praise, and treats only when all four paws are firmly planted on the ground. This positive reinforcement encourages the desired behaviour.
3. Teach and reinforce an incompatible behaviour, such as sitting to greet people. This gives your dog an alternative way to seek attention.

4. Encourage visitors to follow the same protocol to ensure consistency in your dog's training.

Excessive Barking

While barking is a natural form of canine communication, excessive barking can be disruptive and stressful. To address this issue:

1. Identify the root cause of the barking. Common triggers include boredom, anxiety, territoriality, or attention-seeking behaviour.
2. Address the underlying cause directly. For example, provide more mental stimulation for a bored dog or desensitize an anxious dog to its triggers.
3. Teach a "Quiet" command by saying "Quiet" in a calm, firm voice when your dog barks,. then immediately reward silence with treats and praise.
4. Consider using positive interruption techniques, such as making an unusual noise to distract your dog from barking, then rewarding quiet behaviour.

Leash Pulling

Leash pulling can make walks unpleasant and potentially dangerous. To encourage loose-leash walking:

1. Immediately stop walking when your dog begins to pull. This teaches them that pulling doesn't get them where they want to go.
2. Only resume walking when the leash is slack. This reinforces that a loose leash is the key to forward movement.
3. Frequently reward your dog for walking nicely by your

side. Use high-value treats and enthusiastic praise to make walking calmly more rewarding than pulling.

4. Practice in low-distraction environments first, gradually increasing the level of distractions as your dog improves.

Consistency is absolutely crucial in addressing these behavioural issues. Everyone in the household must adhere to the same rules and training techniques to avoid confusing your dog. Patience and persistence are key – behavioural changes take time, but with consistent effort, you'll see significant improvements in your dog's conduct.

Advanced Training: Taking It to the Next Level

Once you've established a solid foundation in basic obedience, it's time to explore the exciting world of advanced training. These more complex exercises not only challenge your dog's mind but also strengthen your bond and provide opportunities for shared activities. Consider venturing into the following advanced training options:

1. Trick Training: This form of training goes beyond basic commands, encouraging your dog to perform impressive feats that showcase their intelligence and agility. Trick training is an excellent way to provide mental stimulation, preventing boredom and reducing the likelihood of destructive behaviours. From teaching your dog to "wave goodbye" to mastering complex sequences like "tidy up toys," the possibilities are endless and highly rewarding for both you and your canine companion.
2. Agility Training: Perfect for high-energy dogs, agility training involves guiding your furry friend through a timed obstacle course. This exhilarating activity not only

provides an excellent physical workout but also hones your dog's focus, improves their coordination, and enhances your communication as a team. From weave poles and tunnels to jumps and see-saws, agility training offers a diverse range of challenges that keep both you and your dog engaged and excited.

3. Scent Work: Tapping into your dog's natural olfactory abilities, scent work training teaches them to identify and locate specific odors. This activity mimics the important jobs of detection dogs and can be a fascinating way to engage your pet's mind. Whether you're hiding treats around the house or participating in formal nose work competitions, this type of training provides mental stimulation while allowing your dog to use their most powerful sense in a structured and rewarding manner.
4. Therapy Dog Training: For dogs with the right temperament – calm, friendly, and patient – therapy dog training can open up a world of opportunities to make a positive impact in your community. This advanced training prepares dogs to provide comfort and support in various settings, such as hospitals, nursing homes, schools, and disaster areas. It requires a high level of obedience, socialization, and adaptability, making it a challenging yet incredibly rewarding pursuit for both dog and owner.

Each of these advanced training options offers unique benefits and challenges. Remember to keep sessions positive, rewarding, and tailored to your dog's individual personality and abilities. With patience and persistence, you'll be amazed at what you and your canine companion can achieve together!

When to Seek Professional Help

While many behavioural issues can be effectively addressed through consistent home training and patience, there are certain situations where seeking professional intervention becomes necessary. It's important to recognize when a problem exceeds your expertise or when your efforts aren't yielding the desired results. In such cases, enlisting the help of a professional dog trainer or behaviourist can be invaluable. These experts possess specialized knowledge and experience to tackle complex canine behavioural challenges. Here are some scenarios that typically warrant professional assistance:

1. Aggression towards people or other animals: This includes any form of growling, snapping, or biting directed at humans or other pets. Professional intervention is crucial to ensure the safety of everyone involved and to address the root cause of the aggressive behaviour.
2. Severe anxiety or phobias: When a dog exhibits intense fear responses to certain stimuli (e.g., thunderstorms, separation from owners, or specific objects), professional help can provide targeted strategies to manage and reduce these anxieties.
3. Compulsive behaviours: These are repetitive, excessive behaviours that seem to serve no apparent purpose, such as excessive licking, tail-chasing, or shadow-chasing. A professional can help identify the underlying cause and develop a tailored treatment plan.
4. Persistent house-training issues: If your dog continues to have accidents indoors despite consistent training efforts, a professional can help identify any medical issues or behavioural factors contributing to the problem.
5. Resource guarding: When a dog becomes overly possessive of food, toys, or other items to the point of aggres-

sion, professional intervention can help modify this potentially dangerous behaviour.

6. Issues that don't improve with consistent training: If you've been diligently working on a behavioural issue for an extended period without seeing significant improvement, it may be time to seek expert advice.

Don't hesitate to consult a professional dog trainer or behaviourist if you find yourself struggling with any of these issues or feeling overwhelmed by your dog's behaviour. These experts can provide personalized strategies, support, and guidance tailored to your specific situation. They can also offer valuable insights into canine psychology and behaviour modification techniques that you may not be aware of. Remember, seeking professional help is not a sign of failure, but rather a responsible step towards ensuring the well-being and happiness of both you and your furry companion. With their expertise, you can overcome challenging behaviours and strengthen the bond with your dog.

Training Throughout Life: An Ongoing Journey

Training is not a finite endeavor that concludes when your puppy reaches adulthood – it's an ongoing, lifelong journey that evolves with your dog's age, experiences, and changing needs. Consistent, regular training sessions throughout your dog's life serve multiple crucial purposes:

1. Mental Stimulation: Regular training exercises keep your dog's mind active and engaged, preventing cognitive decline and reducing the likelihood of boredom-induced behavioural issues.
2. Behavioural Reinforcement: Continuous training helps

reinforce good behaviours and habits, ensuring they remain ingrained even as your dog ages or encounters new situations.

3. Bond Strengthening: The shared experience of learning and accomplishing tasks together deepens the emotional connection between you and your canine companion, fostering mutual trust and understanding.
4. Adaptability: Ongoing training allows you to address new challenges or behaviours that may arise as your dog progresses through different life stages or experiences changes in their environment.

Dedicating even a few minutes each day to training exercises can yield significant, long-lasting benefits for both you and your furry friend. These brief but focused sessions not only maintain and enhance your dog's skills but also provide a structured opportunity for quality time together. This consistent investment in your dog's education and well-being contributes to a harmonious household and a more fulfilling relationship with your canine companion.

Training your dog requires time, patience, and consistency, but the rewards are immeasurable. A well-trained dog is a joy to live with and can accompany you on all sorts of adventures. More importantly, training builds communication and trust between you and your furry friend, strengthening your bond in ways you never imagined.

Every dog is unique. What works for one might not work for another. Be patient with your dog and with yourself. Celebrate the small victories, learn from the setbacks, and above all, enjoy the journey. Your well-mannered canine companion is just around the corner!

8. Grooming Them Right

When you think of a well-groomed dog, you might envision a perfectly coiffed poodle or a silky-smooth golden retriever. But grooming is about so much more than aesthetics. It's a crucial part of your dog's health care routine, a chance to bond with your furry friend, and an opportunity to check for any unusual bumps, lumps, or skin issues. So, let's dive into the world of suds, brushes, and nail clippers!

The Basics: Essential Grooming Tools

Before we delve into the intricacies of grooming, it's essential to equip yourself with the right tools for your canine companion's spa experience. Let's explore the must-have items for your doggy grooming kit:

1. Brush: The cornerstone of any grooming routine, your brush choice depends on your dog's coat type. From slicker brushes for long-haired breeds to bristle brushes for short coats, selecting the right brush is crucial for effective grooming.

2. Comb: An important tool for detangling your pet's fur and adding finishing touches, these combs come in various tooth widths to suit different coat types and grooming needs. Choose one which suits the needs of your pooch.
3. Dog-specific shampoo: Human shampoos can be harsh on your dog's skin, so invest in a quality, pH-balanced dog shampoo tailored to your pup's coat and skin type.
4. Nail clippers or grinder: Regular nail maintenance is vital for your dog's comfort and health. Choose between traditional clippers or an electric grinder based on your preference and your dog's tolerance. It's crucial to understand that nail clipping can often lead to mishaps. Many dogs dislike having their nails trimmed, and novice groomers frequently clip too close to the quick, causing bleeding and injuries. If you lack confidence or your pet strongly resists, consider having this done at a grooming parlor or seek assistance from your veterinarian.
5. Toothbrush and dog toothpaste: Dental hygiene is often overlooked but crucial for your dog's overall health. Use a soft-bristled toothbrush and dog-friendly toothpaste to keep those pearly whites clean and to prevent tartar build up. Unfortunately dogs thrive on a protein heavy diet which only adds to tartar build up in their teeth, so be consistent with dental hygiene.
6. Ear cleaner: Especially important for floppy-eared breeds, a gentle ear cleaner helps prevent infections and remove debris. Ears are also one of the most vulnerable spots for dogs to pick up infections. If you notice your dog scratching their ears frequently, have them checked by the vet immediately.
7. Towels: Have a few absorbent towels on hand for drying

your dog after baths or outdoor adventures.

8. Treats: Never underestimate the power of positive reinforcement! Keep a stash of your dog's favorite treats nearby to reward good behavior during grooming sessions.

Investing in high-quality grooming tools not only enhances the grooming experience for both you and your furry friend but also ensures more effective and comfortable care. While the initial cost might be higher, quality tools often last longer and perform better, making them a worthwhile investment in your dog's health and well-being.

Brushing: The Foundation of Good Grooming

Regular brushing is an essential aspect of dog care, regardless of coat type. This fundamental grooming practice offers numerous benefits for your canine companion:

1. Removal of dead hair and distribution of natural skin oils: Brushing helps to eliminate loose, dead hair from your dog's coat while simultaneously spreading their natural skin oils. This process not only keeps their coat looking clean and shiny but also promotes overall skin health.
2. Prevention of matting and tangling: Regular brushing helps to detangle fur and prevent the formation of painful mats, especially in long-haired breeds. This is particularly important in areas prone to tangling, such as behind the ears, under the legs, and around the tail.
3. Stimulation of blood circulation: The act of brushing gently massages your dog's skin, which can improve blood flow to the skin and hair follicles. This increased circulation can contribute to a healthier coat and may

even aid in reducing inflammation.

4. Early detection of skin issues or parasites: Brushing provides an excellent opportunity to closely examine your dog's skin for any abnormalities, such as lumps, bumps, cuts, or the presence of fleas or ticks. Early detection of these issues can lead to prompt treatment and better overall health outcomes.

The frequency and method of brushing can vary depending on your dog's specific coat type:

- Short, smooth coats: These dogs benefit from weekly brushing using a rubber brush or hound glove. This helps to remove loose hair and distribute skin oils effectively. While these coats may seem low-maintenance, regular brushing is still important for skin health and bonding.
- Medium to long coats: Dogs with longer fur require more frequent attention, typically a few times a week. A slicker brush is excellent for removing tangles and mats, while a metal comb can help work through any remaining knots and add a finishing touch. Pay extra attention to areas prone to matting, such as behind the ears and in the armpits.
- Thick, double coats: Breeds with dense undercoats, such as Huskies, Shih Tzus or German Shepherds, need daily brushing during their heavy shedding seasons (typically spring and fall) and weekly brushing at other times. An undercoat rake is essential for removing loose undercoat hair, followed by a slicker brush to smooth the topcoat. This thorough brushing routine helps prevent matting and reduces the amount of hair shed around your home.

It's crucial to approach brushing as a positive experience for your dog. Start slowly, especially if your dog is new to grooming or has had negative experiences in the past. Use gentle, consistent strokes and offer plenty of praise and treats throughout the process. This positive reinforcement can help your dog associate brushing with pleasant experiences, making future grooming sessions easier and more enjoyable for both of you.

My friend Ravi is a popular dog groomer in Delhi. He's excellent at his job and is favored by many clients for his ability to calm dogs who panic during grooming routines. He's often booked for weeks in advance. Once, he told me about a peculiar case he encountered. A new client came in with their Yorkshire terrier, and to Ravi's astonishment, one of the dog's hind legs had been amputated.

When Ravi asked how it happened, fearing some kind of accident, the client explained that they had been negligent with their pet's grooming, allowing the fur to become matted. They ignored the problem until the matted fur became infected and caused gangrene. Veterinarians had to amputate the leg to prevent the infection from spreading further. This case shows how even seemingly minor negligence can lead to severe problems, even when the issue starts as small as matted fur. If you have a furry breed, please make time for regular grooming—preferably daily.

Remember, patience is key when establishing a brushing routine. Some dogs may take time to adjust, but with consistency and a gentle approach, most dogs learn to enjoy or at least tolerate regular brushing. If you encounter persistent resistance or difficulty, consider consulting a professional groomer or your veterinarian for additional guidance and techniques tailored to your dog's specific needs.

Bathing

1. While dogs don't require baths as frequently as their human counterparts, regular bathing plays a crucial role in maintaining your canine companion's cleanliness, comfort, and overall well-being. The bathing process not only removes dirt, debris, and unpleasant odors but also provides an opportunity to check for any skin abnormalities or parasites. Let's delve into a comprehensive, step-by-step guide to ensure a successful and stress-free bathing experience for both you and your furry friend:
2. Pre-bath preparation: Before introducing your dog to water, thoroughly brush their coat to remove any tangles, mats, or loose fur. This step is particularly important for long-haired breeds as it prevents the formation of tight knots when the fur becomes wet.
3. Setting the stage: Choose a location that's comfortable for both you and your dog. This could be a bathtub, a large sink for smaller breeds, or even outdoors on a warm day. Gather all necessary supplies within arm's reach to avoid leaving your dog unattended during the bath.
4. Water temperature and application: Use lukewarm water to wet your dog's coat thoroughly. The water should be comfortable to the touch, neither too hot nor too cold. Start from the neck and work your way down, being careful to avoid getting water directly in their ears, eyes, or nose.
5. Shampoo selection and application: Choose a dog-specific shampoo that's appropriate for your pet's skin type and any specific needs (e.g., flea control, sensitive skin, etc.). Apply the shampoo starting at the neck and methodically

work your way down the body, paying extra attention to often-neglected areas like the belly, paws, and tail.

6. Gentle massage and lathering: As you apply the shampoo, use your fingers to massage it gently into a rich lather. This not only ensures thorough cleaning but also provides a soothing experience for your dog. Be particularly careful around sensitive areas like the face and ears, using a damp cloth if necessary to clean these parts.
7. Thorough rinsing: Rinse your dog's coat meticulously, ensuring that all shampoo is removed. Any residual shampoo can cause skin irritation and itching. Continue rinsing until the water runs clear, paying special attention to areas where soap can accumulate, such as the armpits, groin, and between the toes.
8. Drying process: Begin by allowing your dog to shake off excess water - it's a natural instinct that helps remove a significant amount of moisture. Then, use a soft, absorbent towel to gently pat and squeeze the fur, rather than rubbing vigorously which can cause tangles.
9. Additional drying for long-haired breeds: For dogs with long or thick coats, you may need to use a blow dryer to ensure they're completely dry. Always use the lowest heat setting and keep the dryer moving to prevent overheating any one area. If your dog is anxious about the noise, consider using a quiet, pet-specific dryer or allow them to air dry in a warm, draft-free area.

It's important to note that the frequency of baths depends on various factors including your dog's breed, lifestyle, and specific health needs. Generally, most dogs benefit from a bath every 4-8 weeks, but this can vary. Some dogs with oily coats may need more frequent baths, while others with dry or sensitive skin might require less frequent bathing. Always consult with your veterinarian to determine the optimal bathing schedule for your individual pet.

While regular bathing is beneficial, over-bathing can strip the natural oils from your dog's coat and skin, potentially leading to dryness, irritation, or other skin issues. Between baths, maintain your dog's hygiene with regular brushing, spot-cleaning as needed, and addressing any specific grooming needs your pet may have. By following these guidelines and paying attention to your dog's individual needs, you'll ensure that bath time becomes a positive, bonding experience that contributes to your pet's overall health and happiness.

Nail Care

If you hear your dog's nails clicking on the floor, it's a clear indication that it's time for a trim. Overgrown nails can cause discomfort for your furry friend and, if left unchecked, may even lead to more serious skeletal issues over time. Proper nail care is an essential aspect of your dog's overall health and well-being. Here's a comprehensive guide on how to approach nail trimming with confidence and care:

1. Choose the right time: Select a moment when your dog is calm and relaxed. This could be after a walk or playtime when they're more likely to be cooperative.
2. Gather the right tools: Invest in high-quality dog nail clippers or a grinder specifically designed for canine use. These tools are crafted to make the process safer and more comfortable for your pet.
3. Understand the anatomy: Familiarize yourself with your dog's nail structure. The quick, a blood vessel inside the nail, should be avoided during trimming. In dogs with light-colored nails, the quick is often visible as a pink area.
4. Master the technique: When trimming, cut at a 45-degree angle, being extremely cautious not to cut into the quick. It's crucial to take small amounts off at a time, rather than trying to achieve the desired length in one cut.
5. Exercise caution: If you're unsure about how much to trim, it's always better to err on the side of caution and take off less. You can always trim a bit more later, but cutting too much can cause pain and bleeding.

6. Be prepared for accidents: Keep styptic powder or cornstarch on hand. In the event that you accidentally cut into the quick and cause bleeding, these substances can help stop the blood flow quickly.
7. Consider desensitization: If your dog is nervous about nail trimming, spend time getting them used to having their paws handled. Offer treats and praise during these sessions to create positive associations.

Nail trimming is a skill that improves with practice. If you find the process stressful for either you or your dog, don't hesitate to seek assistance from a professional groomer or veterinarian. They can demonstrate proper techniques and offer valuable tips to make the experience more manageable. With patience and persistence, nail trimming can become a routine part of your dog's care regimen, ensuring their comfort and mobility for years to come.

Dental Care

Dental health is a critical yet often overlooked aspect of canine care that significantly impacts your dog's overall well-being. Neglecting oral hygiene can lead to a cascade of health issues, ranging from mild discomfort to severe complications. Poor dental care may result in gum disease, tooth decay, and eventual tooth loss. More alarmingly, the bacteria from dental infections can enter the bloodstream, potentially causing damage to vital organs such as the heart, liver, and kidneys. To ensure your furry friend maintains a healthy smile and robust health, consider implementing the following comprehensive dental care routine:

1. Establish a daily tooth-brushing regimen: Aim to brush

your dog's teeth every day, or at the very least, several times a week. Consistency is key in preventing plaque buildup and maintaining oral health.

2. Invest in dog-specific dental products: Use toothbrushes designed for canine mouths and enzymatic toothpaste formulated explicitly for dogs. Never use human toothpaste, as it can contain ingredients harmful to your pet if swallowed.
3. Introduce dental care gradually: Begin by gently massaging your dog's gums with your finger, then progress to a soft cloth, and finally introduce the toothbrush. This gradual approach helps your dog become comfortable with the process.
4. Incorporate dental-friendly toys and treats: Supplement your brushing efforts with specially designed dental chews, toys, or treats that help reduce plaque and tartar buildup.
5. Schedule regular professional cleanings: Even with diligent home care, professional dental cleanings by a veterinarian are essential. These cleanings allow for a thorough examination and removal of hardened tartar that home brushing can't address.

Whether you're starting with a puppy or an older dog, implementing a consistent oral care routine can significantly improve your pet's quality of life and potentially add years to their lifespan. By making dental care a regular part of your dog's grooming routine, you're investing in their long-term health and happiness.

Ear Care

While all dogs require ear care, certain breeds, especially those with floppy or pendulous ears, are more susceptible to ear-related issues. These breeds may trap moisture and debris more easily, creating an environment conducive to infections. To ensure your canine companion's ears remain in optimal condition, follow these guidelines:

1. Conduct weekly ear inspections: Regularly examine your dog's ears for any signs of potential problems. Look out for redness, swelling, unusual odors, or excessive wax buildup. These could be indicators of an underlying issue that requires attention.
2. Implement a proper cleaning routine: Use a veterinarian-approved ear cleaner to maintain ear hygiene. The frequency of cleaning may vary depending on your dog's breed and individual needs. Some dogs may require weekly cleaning, while others might need it less frequently.
3. Master the correct cleaning technique: When cleaning your dog's ears, be gentle and thorough. Apply the cleaner to a cotton ball or soft cloth and wipe the visible parts of the ear canal and flap. Avoid inserting anything deep into the ear canal, as this can cause injury or push debris further inside.
4. Watch for signs of discomfort: Pay attention to behaviors such as excessive head shaking, scratching at the ears, or rubbing the head against furniture. These actions may indicate ear discomfort or the presence of an infection.
5. Seek professional help when necessary: If you notice any signs of infection, such as a foul odor, discharge, or if your dog shows signs of pain when their ears are touched, consult your veterinarian promptly. Early intervention can prevent minor issues from escalating into more seri-

ous problems.

By incorporating these practices into your regular grooming routine, you can help prevent ear infections and ensure your dog's ears remain healthy and comfortable. If you're unsure about the best ear care practices for your specific breed, don't hesitate to seek guidance from your veterinarian or a professional groomer.

Paw Care

Your dog's paw pads, while naturally resilient, require attentive care to maintain their health and comfort, particularly when faced with challenging weather conditions or rough terrains. These tough yet sensitive structures play a crucial role in your dog's mobility and overall well-being. Here's a comprehensive guide on how to keep those precious paws in optimal condition:

1. Conduct regular inspections: Make it a habit to carefully examine your dog's paw pads for any signs of injury or abnormality. Look out for cuts, cracks, bruises, or embedded foreign objects such as small stones or thorns. Early detection of these issues can prevent more serious complications down the line. Paws are also prime locations for ticks and fleas to attach themselves to your dog's body. Regular inspections help catch these pesky parasites early, preventing more serious issues from developing.
2. Practice hot weather precautions: During warm seasons, be mindful of the surfaces your dog walks on. Asphalt and concrete can heat up significantly, potentially causing burns or discomfort to your dog's paw pads. Opt for walks during cooler parts of the day, stick to grassy areas when possible, or consider using protective boots.

3. Implement cold weather protection: Winter brings its own set of challenges for canine paw health. Ice, snow, and de-icing chemicals can all cause irritation or injury. Apply a pet-safe paw balm before walks to create a protective barrier, and consider using specially designed dog booties for extended outdoor activities in cold conditions. After walks, gently wipe your dog's paws to remove any salt or chemicals they may have picked up.
4. Maintain proper grooming: Regular grooming of the paw area is essential for preventing discomfort and potential health issues. Trim the hair between the paw pads if it becomes overgrown, as excessive hair can collect debris, ice, or snow, leading to discomfort or even painful matting. Use blunt-tipped scissors and exercise extreme caution to avoid accidentally nicking the skin.
5. Moisturize dry pads: Just like human skin, dog paw pads can become dry and cracked, especially in extreme weather conditions. Apply a dog-specific paw balm or a small amount of coconut oil to keep the pads supple and prevent painful cracking. Be sure to only use products that are safe for dogs, as they may lick their paws after application.

Special Considerations: Breed-Specific Grooming

Different dog breeds often have unique grooming requirements that cater to their specific physical characteristics and health needs. Understanding and addressing these breed-specific needs is crucial for maintaining your dog's overall health and appearance. Here are some examples illustrating the diverse grooming needs across various breeds:

- Poodles and other non-shedding breeds: These dogs require regular professional grooming to maintain their coats. Their hair grows continuously, similar to human hair, and needs frequent trimming to prevent matting and maintain a neat appearance. Professional groomers can provide specialized cuts that not only keep these dogs looking stylish but also help prevent skin issues that can arise from overgrown coats.
- Bulldogs, Shar Peis, and other wrinkly breeds: The distinctive skin folds of these breeds require extra attention during grooming. These folds can trap moisture and debris, creating an environment conducive to bacterial and yeast growth. Regular cleaning and thorough drying of these areas are essential to prevent skin infections, irritations, and unpleasant odors. Using pet-safe wipes or a soft, damp cloth to clean between the folds, followed by gentle drying, can help maintain skin health.
- Long-eared breeds like Basset Hounds and Cocker Spaniels: These breeds are prone to ear infections due to their ear structure, which can trap moisture and limit air circulation. Extra care should be taken to keep their ears clean and dry. Regular ear checks, gentle cleaning with a veterinarian-approved ear cleaner, and ensuring the ears are thoroughly dried after baths or swimming can help prevent ear infections and other ear-related issues.
- Double-coated breeds like Huskies and German Shepherds: These dogs have a dense undercoat beneath a longer outer coat. They require regular brushing, especially during shedding seasons, to remove loose fur and prevent matting. Using appropriate tools like undercoat rakes

and slicker brushes can help manage their coats effectively and reduce excessive shedding around the house.

- Hairless breeds like Chinese Crested and Xoloitzcuintli: While these dogs don't require traditional coat care, their exposed skin needs special attention. Regular bathing with gentle, moisturizing shampoos, application of sunscreen for outdoor activities, and moisturizing routines are essential to keep their skin healthy and protected from environmental factors.

Given the wide variety of breed-specific grooming needs, it's crucial to research your dog's particular requirements or consult with a professional groomer or veterinarian for personalized advice. They can provide tailored grooming schedules, recommend appropriate tools and products, and offer techniques specific to your dog's breed and individual needs. By understanding and addressing these unique grooming requirements, you can ensure your dog remains healthy, comfortable, and looking their best.

It's important to remember that with consistent effort, patience, and a positive attitude, it can evolve into a rewarding and enjoyable experience for both you and your canine companion. As you practice and refine your grooming techniques, you'll likely find that these sessions not only improve your dog's physical appearance and health but also strengthen the bond between you. Over time, many pet owners discover that grooming becomes a cherished routine, offering a unique opportunity for one-on-one interaction, physical touch, and mutual trust-building with their furry friend.

9. Understanding Your Dog's Behaviour

Wouldn't it be wonderful if our dogs could talk? Imagine the conversations we'd have! While we may not be able to chat with our canine companions in words, the truth is, our dogs are communicating with us all the time. Their language is one of body postures, tail wags, ear positions, and vocalizations. Learning to understand this language is key to a harmonious relationship with your growing dog. So, let's dive into the fascinating world of canine communication and behaviour!

Canine Body Language 101

Dogs are masterful communicators, utilizing their entire bodies to convey a wide range of emotions and intentions. Understanding this intricate language is crucial for any dog owner. Let's delve into a comprehensive guide of key body language cues:

Tail Talk: The Canine Flag

Contrary to popular belief, a wagging tail isn't always a sign of friendliness. The position and speed of the wag can reveal a lot about a dog's state of mind:

- High, stiff wag: This indicates heightened alertness and could potentially signal aggression. The dog is on high alert and may be feeling threatened or territorial.
- Low, gentle wag: This is typically a sign of friendliness and relaxation. The dog is likely feeling content and at ease in its current environment.
- Fast wag with tension: This could indicate anxiety or a state of high arousal. The dog might be excited, but not necessarily in a positive way.
- Circular wag: Often referred to as a 'helicopter tail', this usually indicates extreme happiness and excitement.

Ear Language: Auditory Antennas

A dog's ears are incredibly expressive and can provide valuable insights into their emotional state:

- Ears forward: This suggests the dog is alert and interested in something in their environment. They're actively engaged and processing information.

- Ears pulled back: This can indicate fear or submission. The dog might be feeling uncomfortable or trying to appear non-threatening.
- Ears relaxed: When a dog's ears are in their natural position, neither pricked forward nor pulled back, it usually indicates a calm and content state of mind.
- Ears flicking: Rapid ear movements might suggest the dog is trying to locate the source of a sound or is feeling conflicted about a situation.

Eye Contact: Windows to the Canine Soul

The eyes play a crucial role in canine communication, often revealing a dog's emotional state or intentions:

- Soft gaze: A relaxed, gentle look often indicates affection. This is commonly seen when a dog looks lovingly at their owner.
- Hard stare: An intense, unwavering look can be a threat or challenge. This is not to be confused with the attentive gaze of a dog waiting for a command.
- Avoiding eye contact: This can signify stress or submission. The dog might be trying to diffuse a tense situation or show that they're not a threat.
- Whale eye: When a dog shows the whites of their eyes, often while turning their head away, it can indicate anxiety or discomfort.

Overall Posture: The Big Picture

A dog's overall body posture can provide a wealth of information about their emotional state:

- Relaxed, wiggly body: This usually indicates a friendly and playful mood. The dog is comfortable and may be inviting interaction.
- Stiff, still posture: This suggests the dog is alert and potentially aggressive. They might be assessing a situation they perceive as threatening.
- Lowered body, tail tucked: This posture often indicates fear or submission. The dog is trying to appear smaller and less threatening.
- Play bow: When a dog lowers its front end while keeping its rear end up, it's usually an invitation to play.

It's crucial to consider the context and observe multiple signals together. One isolated cue doesn't tell the whole story. A wagging tail combined with a hard stare and stiff posture, for instance, could indicate a dog is conflicted or potentially aggressive. By learning to read these subtle cues, you'll be better equipped to understand and respond to your canine companion's needs and emotions. Above all, remember that these are only guidelines. Be observant and pay attention to how your dog reacts in different situations and around various people or animals.

Vocalizations: Barks, Whines, and Everything in Between

Dogs possess a diverse and nuanced vocal repertoire, allowing them to communicate a wide range of emotions and needs. Understanding these vocalizations is crucial for interpreting your canine companion's state of mind and responding appropriately.

Let's explore some common canine vocalizations and their potential meanings:

- Barking: This versatile vocalization can convey multiple messages. A sharp, repetitive bark might indicate excitement or alarm, alerting you to potential threats or interesting stimuli in the environment. Alternatively, a persistent, monotonous bark could signify boredom or a demand for attention, suggesting your dog needs mental stimulation or interaction.
- Whining: Often associated with anxiety or discomfort, whining can also serve as a greeting or a polite request. A high-pitched whine might indicate your dog is feeling stressed or unsure, while a softer whine accompanied by a wagging tail could be your dog's way of saying "hello" or asking for something, like food or a walk.
- Growling: While commonly perceived as a warning sign, growling has nuanced meanings in canine communication. A low, rumbling growl typically serves as a caution, signaling discomfort or the need for space. However, don't be alarmed if you hear playful growls during a vigorous game of tug-of-war; many dogs incorporate gentle growls into their play behaviour.
- Howling: This primal vocalization serves multiple purposes in the canine world. Dogs may howl to communicate with distant pack members, respond to high-pitched sounds like sirens, or express feelings of loneliness or anxiety when left alone. Some breeds, like Beagles or Huskies, are more prone to howling than others.

It's important to note that vocalizations alone don't tell the whole story. To accurately interpret your dog's communications, always consider the context of the situation and observe accompanying body language cues. Factors such as ear position, tail movement, and overall posture provide valuable additional information to help you understand what your furry friend is trying to convey.

Common Behaviours Decoded

The Infamous Butt Sniff: A Canine Introduction

Have you ever pondered why our furry friends seem so fascinated by each other's posterior regions? This peculiar behaviour is far more than just a quirky canine habit - it's actually a sophisticated form of information gathering! When dogs engage in this olfactory investigation, they're tapping into a wealth of data transmitted through pheromones released by the anal glands. These chemical signals serve as a comprehensive dossier, revealing intricate details about a fellow canine's age, sex, diet, health status, and even their current emotional state. In essence, this seemingly awkward greeting ritual is akin to a rapid exchange of detailed personal profiles, allowing dogs to quickly assess and understand their peers in ways that go far beyond what meets the human eye.

The Puzzling Head Tilt: More Than Just Adorable

We've all experienced that heart-melting moment when our dogs cock their heads to the side while we're speaking to them. While it undoubtedly makes for endearing photo opportunities, this behaviour serves a much more practical purpose in canine communication. This charming gesture is actually your dog's attempt to enhance their understanding of you and your words.

By tilting their head, they may be adjusting the position of their ears to better localize and interpret the sounds you're making. Additionally, this movement allows them to gain a clearer view of your facial expressions, helping them to pick up on subtle visual cues that accompany your speech. It's a testament to their desire to comprehend and connect with us, showcasing the depth of the human-canine bond.

The Mysterious Circling Before Lying Down: An Ancient Ritual

If you've ever watched your dog perform an elaborate spinning routine before settling down for a nap, you're witnessing a fascinating behavioural relic from their wild ancestors. This seemingly unnecessary ritual actually served crucial purposes in nature. By circling, wild canines would trample down tall grass or snow, creating a more comfortable and level resting spot. This action also served as a way to check for and potentially scare off any small creatures that might be hiding in the vegetation. Moreover, it allowed them to gauge wind direction, ensuring they could position themselves optimally to detect approaching threats through scent. While your domesticated companion may enjoy the luxury of a plush dog bed, this deeply ingrained instinct persists, connecting them to their wild heritage even in the coziest of modern homes.

Understanding Age-Related Behavioural Changes

As your canine companion progresses through various life stages, their behaviour undergoes significant transformations. Understanding these changes is crucial for providing appropriate care and maintaining a strong bond. Let's explore the behavioural characteristics typical of each developmental phase:

Puppy (0-6 months): The Exploratory Phase

- Exhibits boundless curiosity and playfulness, constantly seeking new experiences
- Engages in extensive mouthing and chewing as a means of exploring their environment and alleviating teething discomfort
- Demonstrates a notably short attention span, requiring frequent, brief training sessions

- May undergo fear periods, necessitating gentle exposure to various stimuli for healthy socialization
- Requires consistent potty training and basic obedience instruction

Adolescent (6-18 months): The Challenging Phase

- Begins testing boundaries, often challenging established rules and commands
- Experiences a surge in energy levels, potentially leading to increased mischievous behaviour
- May exhibit heightened reactivity or fearfulness, requiring patient guidance and positive reinforcement
- Undergoes sexual maturity if not spayed/neutered, potentially leading to hormone-driven behaviours
- Benefits greatly from continued training and mental stimulation to channel excess energy

Adult (18 months-7 years): The Stability Phase

- Develops a more settled and consistent personality
- Demonstrates reliable behaviour patterns, especially with continued reinforcement of training
- Enters their prime years for learning advanced commands and participating in various activities
- May excel in specific roles or tasks, such as agility, obedience, or therapy work
- Requires regular exercise and mental stimulation to maintain physical and psychological well-being

Senior (7+ years): The Golden Phase

- Experiences a gradual decrease in physical activity levels and energy
- May exhibit cognitive changes, such as confusion or alterations in sleep patterns
- Often becomes more set in their ways, potentially less adaptable to changes in routine
- Requires adjustments in diet, exercise, and healthcare to accommodate age-related needs
- Benefits from gentler activities and increased comfort measures to ensure quality of life

Remember, these are general guidelines, and individual dogs may progress through these stages at different rates. Factors such as breed, size, and overall health can influence the timing and extent of these behavioural changes. Maintaining open communication with your veterinarian and staying attuned to your dog's unique needs will help ensure a happy, healthy life throughout all stages of development.

When Canine Behaviour Becomes Challenging: Recognizing and Addressing Problematic Patterns

While dogs naturally exhibit a wide range of behaviours, certain actions can become problematic when they interfere with daily life or pose risks to the dog's well-being or that of others. It's crucial for dog owners to recognize these issues and understand their potential root causes. Let's explore some common behavioural challenges and their underlying factors:

1. Excessive vocalization: Persistent barking, howling, or whining can stem from various sources, including boredom, anxiety, territorial instincts, or learned patterns of

attention-seeking. This behaviour may also indicate underlying health issues or environmental stressors that require attention.

2. Destructive tendencies: Chewing, digging, or scratching beyond normal exploratory behaviour can be attributed to several factors. In puppies, teething discomfort often drives this behaviour. For adult dogs, it may signal anxiety, insufficient mental stimulation, or attempts to alleviate stress. Sometimes, it's simply a learned behaviour that has been inadvertently reinforced.
3. Separation-related issues: Dogs experiencing distress when left alone may exhibit behaviours such as excessive vocalization, destructiveness, or inappropriate elimination. This anxiety often stems from a lack of gradual conditioning to solitude, past traumatic experiences, or an overly dependent relationship with their human companions.
4. Aggressive displays: Aggression in dogs can manifest in various forms, from growling and snapping to full-blown attacks. The roots of such behaviour are complex and may include fear, resource guarding instincts, lack of proper socialization, pain or discomfort, or a history of negative experiences. It's crucial to identify the specific triggers and contexts of aggressive behaviour to address it effectively.
5. Compulsive behaviours: Some dogs develop repetitive actions like excessive licking, tail-chasing, or shadow-chasing. These behaviours often start as normal activities but become exaggerated and difficult to interrupt. They may be triggered by stress, anxiety, or even neurological issues.

It's important to note that addressing these behavioural challenges requires patience, consistency, and often professional guidance. Punishment-based approaches are generally ineffective and can exacerbate the problem by increasing fear and anxiety. Instead, focus on positive reinforcement techniques and addressing the underlying causes of the behaviour.

If you find yourself grappling with any of these issues, don't hesitate to seek help from a qualified professional. A certified dog trainer or animal behaviourist can provide tailored strategies to modify problematic behaviours and strengthen the bond between you and your canine companion. Remember, early intervention is key to preventing these behaviours from becoming deeply ingrained habits.

Understanding your dog's behaviour is like learning a new language. By learning to read your dog's signals and understanding their needs at different life stages, you're setting the foundation for a strong, trusting relationship.

Every dog is an individual with their own unique personality and quirks. What's normal for one dog might be unusual for another. The key is to observe, learn, and respond to your particular pup's needs and communications.

As you continue on this journey with your growing dog, stay curious, patient, and open-minded. Your efforts to understand your canine companion will be rewarded with a deeper bond and a more harmonious household. After all, isn't that what having a dog is all about?

10. Daily Life With Your Dog

Living with a dog is an adventure filled with wagging tails and unconditional love. But it's also about the everyday routines, the small moments, and the daily decisions that shape your life together. In this chapter, we'll explore how to seamlessly integrate your furry friend into your daily life, creating a harmonious household where both you and your dog can thrive.

Establishing a Routine

Dogs are creatures of habit, thriving on predictability and structure in their daily lives. A well-established routine provides them with a sense of security and clarity about what to expect throughout the day. This consistency not only helps reduce anxiety but also aids in behavior management and training. Let's explore a comprehensive daily schedule that caters to your canine companion's needs:

1. Early Morning: Start the day with a refreshing walk and potty break, allowing your dog to relieve themselves and get some gentle exercise.

2. Breakfast Time: Serve your furry friend their morning meal, maintaining a consistent feeding schedule to regulate their digestion and energy levels.
3. Morning Exercise: Engage in a vigorous play session or structured exercise routine to burn off excess energy and stimulate your dog both physically and mentally.
4. Mid-morning Break: If possible, arrange for a quick potty break or short walk to keep your dog comfortable and maintain their bathroom habits.
5. Afternoon Activity: Plan another walk or interactive play session to break up the day and provide additional physical and mental stimulation.
6. Evening Meal: Serve dinner at a regular time, reinforcing the routine and ensuring your dog's nutritional needs are met.
7. Evening Outing: Take your four-legged friend for their final walk of the day, allowing them to stretch their legs and take care of any last-minute bathroom needs.
8. Bedtime Ritual: Establish a calming pre-sleep routine, which might include a quiet play session, grooming, or simply some cuddle time to help your dog wind down for the night.

While maintaining a consistent schedule is ideal, it's essential to remember that life doesn't always follow a strict timetable. Flexibility within your routine is crucial. Dogs are adaptable creatures, and they will adjust to occasional changes as long as their fundamental needs are consistently met. The key is to provide a stable framework that can bend without breaking, ensuring your furry companion feels secure and well-cared for, even when unexpected events disrupt the usual flow of your day.

The Art of Leaving and Returning Home

For many dogs, the moments when their human leaves or returns home are emotionally intense and can significantly impact their behavior and well-being. These transitions often trigger a range of reactions, from anxiety to over-excitement. To ensure these daily occurrences are as smooth and stress-free as possible for both you and your furry companion, consider implementing the following strategies:

Departures: Easing the Goodbye

1. Keep farewells low-key and brief to minimize anxiety buildup. Avoid lengthy, emotional goodbyes that may inadvertently signal to your dog that something is wrong.
2. Provide a special toy or long-lasting treat as you leave. This positive association can help redirect your dog's attention and create a pleasant distraction.
3. Gradually accustom your dog to your absences by practicing short departures. Start with brief periods and slowly increase the duration to build your dog's confidence and reduce separation anxiety.
4. Establish a consistent pre-departure routine, such as picking up your keys or putting on your shoes, to help your dog anticipate and accept your leaving.

Returns: Managing the Reunion

1. When you return home, greet your dog calmly and with minimal fuss. This approach helps avoid reinforcing

over-excitement and jumping behaviors.

2. Wait until your dog has settled down before engaging in enthusiastic play or showing affection. This teaches them that calm behavior is rewarded.
3. Consider taking your dog for a walk or engaging in a play session shortly after your return. This helps release any pent-up energy from their time alone and reinforces positive associations with your homecoming.
4. Use this opportunity to reinforce basic obedience commands, asking your dog to sit or stay before receiving attention, which helps maintain good manners.

As with most things dog related, consistency is key in implementing these strategies. With time and patience, you can help your dog develop a more relaxed attitude towards your comings and goings, creating a happier and more balanced home environment for both of you.

Balancing Work and Dog: The Modern Pet Parent's Challenge

For many of us, the necessity of leaving our canine companions at home while we pursue our careers is an unavoidable aspect of modern life. However, this separation need not be a source of stress or guilt. With thoughtful planning and implementation of various strategies, we can ensure that our furry friends remain content, stimulated, and well-cared for during our absence. Here are some comprehensive approaches to maintain your dog's happiness and well-being:

1. Engage Professional Services: Consider hiring a reputable dog walker or enrolling your pet in a high-quality dog-

gy daycare facility. These options provide your dog with essential physical exercise, social interaction, and mental stimulation during the workday.

2. Provide Engaging Toys: Invest in a variety of puzzle toys, interactive feeders, or frozen Kong toys filled with dog-safe treats. These mentally stimulating items can keep your dog occupied for extended periods, alleviating boredom and potential anxiety.
3. Create a Comforting Atmosphere: Leave a radio or television on at a low volume to provide soothing background noise. This can help mask potentially startling outside sounds and create a sense of company for your dog.
4. Explore Canine Companionship: If your lifestyle and resources permit, contemplate adopting a second dog to provide companionship. However, this decision should not be taken lightly and requires careful consideration of your ability to care for multiple pets.
5. Utilize Technology: Set up a pet camera with two-way communication and treat-dispensing capabilities. This allows you to check in on your dog, offer reassuring words, and even provide rewards remotely throughout the day.
6. Establish a Robust Exercise Routine: Remember the adage, "a tired dog is a good dog." Implement a consistent exercise regimen that includes vigorous activity before and after your workday. This helps expend excess energy and promotes better behavior and relaxation during your absence.

By implementing these strategies, you can create a nurturing environment that supports your dog's physical and emotional well-being, even when you can't be there in person. Remember, every dog is unique, so be prepared to adjust your approach based on your pet's individual needs and responses.

Mealtime Manners: Creating Positive Feeding Routines

Feeding time is not just about nourishment; it's a prime opportunity to reinforce positive behaviors and strengthen your bond with your canine companion. Transform mealtime into an enriching experience with these comprehensive tips:

1. Establish Consistent Feeding Schedule: Set regular mealtimes that align with your dog's age, health needs, and your daily routine. This predictability helps regulate their digestive system and can aid in housetraining efforts.
2. Leverage Mealtimes for Training: Use these moments as valuable training opportunities. Incorporate commands like "sit," "stay," or "wait" before placing the bowl down. This not only reinforces obedience but also teaches patience and impulse control.
3. Introduce Mental Stimulation: Consider using puzzle feeders or interactive food toys to make meals more engaging. These tools can slow down fast eaters, provide mental stimulation, and tap into your dog's natural foraging instincts.
4. Practice Mealtime Supervision: Always oversee feeding sessions, especially in multi-pet households. This allows you to monitor each pet's eating habits, prevent food aggression, and ensure everyone gets their fair share.
5. Implement a "Clean Plate" Policy: Remove food bowls between meals to establish a routine and discourage grazing. This practice can help maintain a healthy weight and

make it easier to monitor your dog's appetite and food intake.

6. Portion Control is Key: Measure your dog's food accurately to maintain a healthy weight. Consult with your veterinarian to determine the appropriate portion size based on your dog's age, breed, size, and activity level.
7. Create a Calm Feeding Environment: Designate a quiet, low-traffic area for mealtimes. This can reduce stress and distractions, allowing your dog to focus on their meal and enjoy it fully.

By implementing these strategies, you can transform the simple act of feeding into a rewarding ritual that nourishes both body and mind, further strengthening the special bond you share with your furry friend.

Exercise and Play: Keeping the Zoomies at Bay

Regular exercise and play are essential components of your dog's overall health and happiness, contributing significantly to their physical fitness and mental acuity. The amount of daily activity your canine companion requires can vary widely, typically ranging from a minimum of 30 minutes to as much as 2 hours or more. This variation depends on several factors, including your dog's age, breed characteristics, individual energy levels, and overall health status. To ensure your furry friend receives a well-rounded exercise regimen, consider incorporating a diverse array of activities into their routine, such as:

1. Brisk walks or invigorating jogs through your neighborhood or local park
2. Engaging games of fetch with a ball or frisbee, promoting

both physical exertion and bonding

3. Spirited tug-of-war sessions, which can help strengthen your dog's muscles and satisfy their natural instincts
4. Swimming exercises, particularly beneficial for low-impact, full-body workouts
5. Challenging agility courses, either professionally designed or creatively constructed at home, to enhance coordination and problem-solving skills
6. Stimulating hide-and-seek games using treats or favorite toys, encouraging your dog to use their nose and cognitive abilities

It's crucial to recognize that mental stimulation is equally important as physical exercise in maintaining your dog's overall well-being. To this end, make sure to weave training sessions, interactive puzzle toys, and novel experiences into your dog's daily routine. These mentally engaging activities can help prevent boredom, reduce anxiety, and foster a more balanced and content canine companion.

Sleep Arrangements: To Share or Not to Share?

The sleeping arrangements for your canine companion are a personal decision that depends on various factors, including your lifestyle, preferences, and your dog's needs. Whether you choose to share your bed, have your dog sleep in their own bed within your room, or designate a separate sleeping area elsewhere in the house, the most crucial aspect is maintaining consistency in your chosen arrangement. This consistency helps establish a routine and provides your dog with a sense of security and comfort.

If you opt for separate sleeping quarters for your furry friend, it's essential to create an inviting and cozy environment. Consider the following tips to make their sleeping area as comfortable as possible:

- Invest in a high-quality, appropriately sized dog bed that supports your pet's body and accommodates their preferred sleeping position.
- Place familiar toys and items with your scent nearby to provide comfort and reduce anxiety.
- Use soft blankets or cushions to create a nest-like atmosphere that appeals to your dog's natural instincts.
- Ensure the sleeping area is in a quiet, draft-free location to promote restful sleep.
- Consider using pheromone diffusers or calming aids if your dog experiences nighttime anxiety.

Regardless of where your dog sleeps, the goal is to create a safe, comfortable space that promotes quality rest and reinforces the bond between you and your canine companion.

Navigating Social Situations: Your Dog in a Human World

Integrating your canine companion into your social life requires thoughtful consideration and planning. Here are some comprehensive tips to ensure harmonious interactions:

1. Invest time in training your dog to greet guests with politeness and restraint. This includes teaching them to sit calmly, avoid jumping, and wait for permission before approaching visitors.
2. Develop a strategic plan for occasions when non-dog-friendly guests visit. This might involve creating a comfortable, separate space for your dog or arranging for them to stay with a trusted friend or family member.
3. Conduct thorough research to identify and compile a list of dog-friendly establishments in your area, including restaurants, cafes, and outdoor venues. This preparation allows for spontaneous outings without compromising your dog's inclusion.
4. Carefully assess and respect your dog's individual comfort level in various social situations. Pay close attention to their body language and behavior cues, and avoid forcing interactions that may cause stress or anxiety.
5. Gradually expose your dog to different social environments through positive experiences. Start with calm, controlled situations and progressively introduce more

challenging scenarios as your dog's confidence grows.

6. Educate your friends and family about your dog's specific needs and boundaries. This proactive approach helps create a supportive network that understands and respects your dog's presence in social gatherings.

Home Alone: Keeping Your Dog Safe and Happy

When circumstances necessitate leaving your canine companion alone, it's crucial to create an environment that prioritizes both their safety and comfort. Here are some comprehensive strategies to ensure your dog's well-being during your absence:

1. Regularly assess and dog-proof your living space: Conduct thorough inspections to identify and eliminate potential hazards such as exposed wires, toxic plants, or small objects that could be swallowed.
2. Provide an array of engaging toys and puzzles: Offer a diverse selection of interactive toys, chew items, and puzzle feeders to keep your dog mentally stimulated and physically occupied throughout your absence.
3. Implement crate training for shorter periods: Consider introducing a crate as a safe, comfortable space for your dog during brief absences. Ensure the crate is appropriately sized and filled with cozy bedding and familiar items.
4. Ensure constant access to fresh, clean water: Place multiple water bowls throughout your home to guarantee your dog stays hydrated, regardless of their location within the house.
5. Create a soothing auditory environment: Leave a radio, television, or white noise machine on at a low volume

to provide comforting background sounds that can help mask potentially startling noises from outside.

6. Utilize baby gates or designated areas strategically: Employ baby gates or create specific zones within your home to restrict access to certain areas, balancing your dog's freedom of movement with the need to protect both your belongings and your pet's safety.
7. Consider temperature control: Ensure your home's climate remains comfortable for your dog, adjusting thermostats or providing fans as needed to maintain an ideal temperature range.
8. Set up a pet camera: Install a pet camera with two-way communication capabilities, allowing you to monitor your dog's behavior and offer reassuring words if necessary.

Downtime is equally important

While routines and activities are important, don't underestimate the value of quiet time together. Whether it's cuddling on the couch or simply being in the same room while you work, these calm moments can strengthen your bond.

Adapting to Change

Life is full of unexpected twists and turns, and there will inevitably be periods when your carefully crafted routine faces disruption. These changes could stem from various life events, such as relocating to a new home, welcoming a new family member, experiencing shifts in your work schedule, or dealing with unforeseen circumstances. During these transitional phases, it's crucial to remember that your canine companion may also feel the effects of these changes. To ensure your dog's well-being and maintain a sense of stability, consider the following strategies:

1. Strive to preserve as much of your dog's established routine as possible, even amidst the chaos. This consistency can serve as an anchor for your furry friend during uncertain times.
2. Offer an extra dose of comfort, reassurance, and attention to your dog. This can help alleviate any anxiety or stress they might be experiencing due to the changes in their environment or daily life.

3. Be vigilant for signs of stress or anxiety in your dog, such as excessive panting, pacing, or changes in appetite. If these symptoms persist, consider employing calming aids like pheromone diffusers, anxiety wraps, or natural supplements, after consulting with your veterinarian.
4. Amidst the whirlwind of change, it's easy to become overwhelmed. However, it's crucial to remain mindful of your dog's fundamental needs. Ensure that their regular feeding schedule, exercise routines, and bathroom breaks are maintained as much as possible.
5. Create a designated "safe space" for your dog within your home, complete with their favorite toys, bed, and familiar scents. This area can serve as a retreat where they can relax and feel secure during times of change.

As a pack animal, your dog looks to you for guidance and stability. By maintaining a calm demeanour and addressing their needs consistently, you can help your furry companion navigate through life's transitions with greater ease and comfort.

Embracing your dog as a part of your daily life isn't always easy, but the rewards – loyalty, love, and companionship – are immeasurable. Here's to the beautiful, ordinary days that make up an extraordinary life with your canine best friend!

11. Preparing For Unforeseen Challenges

Like any worthwhile adventure, having a dog comes with its share of challenges. From behavioral issues to health concerns, from lifestyle changes to unexpected situations, being a dog parent means being prepared to face and overcome a variety of hurdles. In this chapter, we'll explore common challenges dog owners face and provide strategies to navigate them successfully.

Behavioural Challenges: When Good Dogs Act Out

Even the most well-behaved dogs can occasionally exhibit problematic behaviors. These challenges are a normal part of dog ownership and can often be addressed with patience, consistency, and the right approach. In this section, we'll explore some common behavioral issues that dog owners might encounter and provide detailed strategies for managing and resolving them effectively:

1. Excessive Barking

- Identify the root cause of the barking (e.g., boredom, anxiety, territorial behavior, attention-seeking)
- Address the underlying issue through targeted interventions (e.g., increased exercise, mental stimulation, desensitization training)
- Teach and reinforce a "quiet" command using positive reinforcement techniques
- Implement environmental management strategies to reduce triggers
- Consider anti-bark devices as a last resort, under professional guidance

2. Separation Anxiety

- Implement a gradual desensitization program to acclimate your dog to being alone
- Provide engaging toys, puzzles, and long-lasting treats to keep your dog occupied
- Create a calm, safe space for your dog when you're away
- Consider using calming aids such as pheromone diffusers, anxiety wraps, or calming music
- Practice short departures and returns to build your dog's confidence
- In severe cases, consult with a professional behaviorist for a tailored treatment plan

3. Leash Reactivity

- Identify specific triggers that cause reactivity (e.g., other dogs, people, vehicles)
- Implement a structured desensitization and counter-con-

ditioning program

- Teach and reinforce focus commands to redirect your dog's attention
- Use positive reinforcement techniques to reward calm behavior around triggers
- Practice management strategies such as changing walking routes or times to reduce exposure to triggers
- Consider working with a professional trainer experienced in reactive dog rehabilitation

4. Resource Guarding

- Never punish guarding behaviour, as this can escalate the issue
- Teach and reinforce "leave it" and "drop it" commands

using positive reinforcement

- Practice trading exercises, offering high-value treats in exchange for guarded items
- Implement management strategies to prevent access to commonly guarded items
- Work on building overall trust and positive associations with human presence near resources
- For severe or potentially dangerous cases, consult a professional behaviorist for a comprehensive treatment plan

Addressing behavioral issues requires patience, consistency, and often professional guidance. Each dog is unique, and what works for someone may not work for another. Always prioritize your dog's emotional well-being and safety when implementing any behaviour modification strategies.

Lifestyle Challenges: Adapting to Life Changes

Life is a dynamic journey, and the ebbs and flows of our personal circumstances can significantly impact our ability to care for our canine companions. As responsible dog owners, it's crucial to anticipate and prepare for these changes, ensuring that our furry friends remain happy, healthy, and well-adjusted throughout life's transitions. In this section, we'll explore some common scenarios that dog owners may face and provide comprehensive strategies for navigating these changes while maintaining the well-being of both you and your beloved pet.

1. Moving to a New Home

- Gradually introduce your dog to the new space, allowing them to explore at their own pace
- Maintain as much of your old routine as possible to provide a sense of stability and familiarity
- Be patient with adjustment periods, understanding that some dogs may take longer to acclimate than others
- Update ID tags and microchip information to ensure your dog can be safely returned if they get lost in the new area
- Create a comfortable, familiar space in the new home with your dog's favorite toys, bed, and belongings
- Explore the new neighborhood together, helping your dog become familiar with new sights, sounds, and smells

2. New Baby in the Family

- Gradually introduce baby-related items before the arrival to help your dog adjust to new scents and sounds
- Maintain your dog's routine as much as possible to minimize stress and anxiety
- Never leave the baby and dog unsupervised, prioritizing safety for both
- Ensure your dog has a quiet space to retreat to when they need a break from the new activity
- Involve your dog in baby-related activities to foster positive associations
- Consider professional training or behavior modification if your dog shows signs of stress or anxiety

3. Financial Strain

- Research and utilize low-cost veterinary clinics for routine care and vaccinations
- Consider pet insurance before health issues arise to potentially offset future costs
- Learn to groom your dog at home, saving money on professional grooming services
- Make homemade toys and treats using safe, dog-friendly ingredients
- Explore community resources such as pet food banks or assistance programs
- Consider bartering pet-related services with other dog owners in your community

4. Changes in Work Schedule

- Gradually adjust your dog's routine to align with your

new schedule

- Explore options for dog walkers, daycare, or pet sitters if needed
- Increase mental stimulation through puzzle toys when you're away for longer periods
- Make the most of your time together by engaging in quality activities and exercise

While these life changes can be challenging, they also present opportunities to strengthen your bond with your dog. With patience and planning, you and your furry friend can successfully navigate these transitions together, emerging with an even stronger relationship on the other side.

Environmental Challenges: Dealing with the Outdoors

The great outdoors can present various challenges for dog owners. Mother Nature often throws unexpected situations our way, requiring us to be prepared and adaptable. In this section, we'll explore some common environmental challenges and provide comprehensive strategies to navigate them effectively, ensuring both you and your furry companion can enjoy outdoor adventures safely:

1. Extreme Weather Conditions

Hot weather:

- Provide ample shade and fresh water to prevent dehydration
- Avoid walks during the hottest parts of the day, typically

between 10 AM and 4 PM

- Consider cooling accessories like bandanas or mats for added comfort
- Be vigilant for signs of heat exhaustion, such as excessive panting or lethargy

Cold weather:

- Invest in properly fitted doggy boots to protect paws from ice and salt
- Use insulated coats or sweaters for breeds with short or thin coats
- Limit outdoor exposure, especially for smaller or senior dogs
- Monitor for signs of hypothermia, including shivering or sluggishness
- Be aware of breed-specific sensitivities to extreme temperatures
- Always have a backup plan or indoor alternatives for exercise during harsh weather

2. Wildlife Encounters

Preventive measures:

- Keep your dog on a leash in areas known for wildlife activity
- Use a harness for better control during unexpected encounters
- Avoid walking during dawn and dusk when many wild animals are most active

Training and preparedness:

- Teach and reinforce a reliable recall command for emergencies
- Practice "leave it" and "stay" commands to prevent chase behaviors
- Familiarize yourself with local wildlife and appropriate response strategies

Specific wildlife considerations:

- Snakes: Learn to identify venomous species in your area and avoid their habitats
- Insects: For insect stings, remove the stinger if still attached on the skin of your dog. Apply ice-pack or appropriate skin creams if available.
- Monkeys: Distract with sound and shiny objects and keep your dog on a leash. Scratches and bites can often turn infectious.

Post-encounter actions:

- Check your dog thoroughly for injuries after any wildlife encounter
- Report dangerous wildlife sightings to local authorities

3. Toxic Plants and Hazardous Substances

Plant awareness:

- Research and learn to identify common toxic plants in your local area
- Be particularly cautious of plants like lilies, azaleas, and sago palms
- Consider removing dangerous plants from your yard or garden

Household and outdoor hazards:

- Secure potentially harmful substances out of your dog's reach
- Be mindful of seasonal hazards like antifreeze or fertilizers
- Use pet-safe alternatives for household cleaning and lawn care when possible

By being proactive and prepared for these environmental challenges, you can ensure that outdoor experiences with your dog remain safe, enjoyable, and enriching for both of you. Remember, knowledge and preparation are key to confidently navigating the beautiful yet sometimes unpredictable natural world with your canine companion.

Social Challenges: Navigating a Human World

Navigating the social aspects of dog ownership can sometimes be challenging, as interactions with other humans can present unique obstacles. In this section, we'll explore some common social situations that dog owners may encounter and provide comprehensive strategies for handling them effectively:

1. Dealing with Unfriendly Neighbors

- Promptly address any legitimate concerns raised by neighbours, such as excessive barking or property damage
- Familiarize yourself with local laws and regulations regarding dog ownership to ensure compliance
- Maintain open communication with neighbors to foster understanding and resolve issues amicably

- Consider professional mediation services for ongoing disputes that seem difficult to resolve
- Implement proactive measures, such as soundproofing or additional training, to minimize potential conflicts

2. Navigating Dog-Unfriendly Environments

- Conduct thorough research to identify dog-friendly alternatives for dining, travel, and housing in your area
- Actively advocate for more inclusive, dog-friendly policies within your community through local government channels
- Cultivate a supportive network of dog-loving friends and fellow pet owners for social interactions and mutual support
- Explore creative solutions, such as pet-sitting services or doggy daycare, when facing temporary dog-unfriendly situations
- Educate others about the benefits of dog-friendly environments to promote positive change

3. Handling Unwanted Advice or Criticism

- Maintain a calm and confident demeanour when faced with unsolicited opinions about your dog or your pet parenting choices
- Educate yourself thoroughly on dog behavior, training methods, and health to confidently explain and justify your decisions
- Develop the ability to discern between constructive feedback and unnecessary criticism, engaging or disengaging

accordingly

- Practice assertive communication techniques to politely but firmly set boundaries with overzealous advice-givers
- Seek support from like-minded dog owners or professionals when dealing with persistent criticism or doubt

Navigating these social challenges is an integral part of responsible dog ownership. By approaching these situations with patience, understanding, and a willingness to communicate, you can create a more harmonious environment for both you and your canine companion.

Emergency Preparedness

As dog owners, we hope never to face an emergency situation with our beloved pets. However, being prepared for the unexpected is a crucial part of responsible pet ownership. From natural disasters to sudden health crises, having a plan in place can make all the difference in keeping your furry friend safe. In this chapter, we'll explore how to prepare for various emergencies and how to act swiftly and effectively when they occur.

Creating an Emergency Kit: Your Canine Go-Bag

Every responsible dog owner should be prepared for emergencies by having a well-stocked and readily accessible emergency kit. This crucial "go-bag" for your canine companion should contain the following essential items:

1. Sufficient food and water to sustain your dog for at least 72 hours (3-day supply)

2. Collapsible or lightweight food and water bowls for easy portability
3. A two-week supply of any medications your dog regularly takes, along with clear dosage instructions
4. A comprehensive first-aid kit tailored for canine needs (we'll provide a detailed list of contents later in this chapter)
5. A sturdy leash, a properly fitting collar, and up-to-date ID tags with your current contact information
6. Printed copies of your dog's medical records, including vaccination history and any chronic conditions
7. Multiple recent, clear photographs of your dog from various angles to aid in identification if separated
8. A familiar blanket or bedding item to provide comfort and warmth in stressful situations
9. An ample supply of waste bags for maintaining hygiene during extended periods away from home
10. Your dog's favorite toy or a cherished comfort item to help alleviate anxiety in unfamiliar environments

To ensure your emergency kit remains effective, store it in an easily accessible location, clearly labeled for quick retrieval. Make a habit of reviewing and updating the contents every six months, replacing any expired items, updating documents, and adjusting supplies based on your dog's changing needs. By maintaining this level of preparedness, you'll be ready to face unexpected situations with confidence, knowing you have the essentials to keep your furry friend safe and comfortable.

First Aid Essentials: Be Your Dog's First Responder

A comprehensive first aid kit is an essential component of responsible dog ownership. Ensure your kit includes the following items:

1. Sterile gauze pads and rolls for wound dressing
2. Medical-grade adhesive tape for securing bandages
3. Sharp, sterile scissors for cutting bandages or trimming fur around wounds
4. Fine-tipped tweezers for removing splinters or ticks
5. Antiseptic wipes or solution for cleaning wounds
6. Sterile saline solution for flushing eyes or wounds
7. Disposable non-latex gloves to maintain hygiene during treatment
8. Digital rectal thermometer specifically designed for pets
9. Oral syringe or turkey baster for administering liquid medications
10. Self-adhering bandage wrap (vet wrap) for securing dressings
11. 3% hydrogen peroxide solution (use only under veterinary guidance to induce vomiting in specific poisoning cases)
12. Activated charcoal tablets or liquid (administer only under veterinary supervision for certain types of poisoning)
13. Styptic powder to stop bleeding from minor cuts, such as torn nails
14. Petroleum jelly for various uses, including protecting paw pads
15. Blanket or towel for warmth or as a makeshift stretcher

It's crucial to not only stock these items but also to understand how to use them properly. Consider enrolling in a pet-specific first aid course to gain hands-on experience and confidence in emergency situations. Remember to regularly check and replenish your kit, ensuring all items are within their expiration dates and in good condition. By being prepared and knowledgeable, you'll be better equipped to provide immediate care for your furry friend in times of need.

Natural Disaster Preparedness: When Mother Nature Strikes

Natural disasters can strike unexpectedly, and their impact varies greatly depending on your geographical location. To ensure the safety of both you and your canine companion during such events, it's crucial to have a comprehensive preparedness plan tailored to your region's specific risks. Here's an in-depth guide on how to prepare for various natural disasters:

1. Evacuation Plan: Your Lifeline in Crisis

- Research and document multiple pet-friendly evacuation routes, considering potential road closures or hazards
- Compile an extensive list of pet-friendly shelters, including their contact information and any specific requirements
- Create a comprehensive directory of pet-friendly hotels or lodging options in various directions and distances from your home
- Establish a network of out-of-area contacts who can assist with coordination and information relay during emergencies
- Prepare a detailed evacuation checklist to ensure no essential items or steps are overlooked in the heat of the

moment

Stay-at-Home Plan: Fortifying Your Home Front

- Conduct a thorough assessment of your home to identify the safest room, considering factors like structural integrity and accessibility
- Create a comprehensive inventory of emergency supplies needed for both you and your dog, and maintain a generous stockpile in your designated safe room
- Install and regularly test multiple methods of receiving emergency alerts, such as battery-powered radios, smartphone apps, and local warning systems
- Develop a home safety plan that includes strategies for securing loose objects, protecting windows, and managing utilities during various types of disasters
- Consider investing in a generator or alternative power source to maintain essential services during extended outages

3. General Tips: Enhancing Overall Preparedness

- Regularly update your dog's microchip information, ensuring all contact details are current and comprehensive
- Place clearly visible "Pets Inside" stickers on all entry points of your home, specifying the number and types of pets for rescuers
- Conduct frequent, realistic evacuation drills with your entire family, including your dog, to familiarize everyone with the process
- Create and maintain a detailed pet emergency kit, includ-

ing food, water, medications, and comfort items, updating it seasonally
- Establish relationships with neighbors or nearby friends who can check on or evacuate your dog if you're unable to reach home during an emergency
- Stay informed about your area's specific disaster risks and tailor your preparedness efforts accordingly, seeking guidance from local emergency management offices

By meticulously preparing for various scenarios and regularly reviewing your plans, you'll be better equipped to protect your furry friend when nature unleashes its fury. Thorough preparation can make all the difference in ensuring the safety and well-being of your beloved canine companion during challenging times.

Health Emergencies: Recognizing and Responding

Being able to recognize and respond to common health emergencies is crucial for every dog owner. Familiarize yourself with these critical situations and their appropriate responses:

1. Heatstroke: A Potentially Fatal Condition

Signs: Watch for excessive panting, drooling, lethargy, vomiting, and bright red gums. In severe cases, seizures or collapse may occur.

Response: Immediately move your dog to a cool, shaded area. Apply cool (not cold) water to their body, especially the neck, armpits, and groin areas. Use a fan if available to increase air circulation. Offer small amounts of water to drink. Even if your dog seems to recover, seek immediate veterinary care as complications can develop hours later.

2. Poisoning: Swift Action is Essential

Signs: Symptoms can vary widely depending on the toxin, but may include vomiting, diarrhea, seizures, unusual behavior, drooling, loss of appetite, and lethargy.

Response: If you suspect poisoning, call pet poison control or your veterinarian immediately. Have information ready about what your dog may have ingested, how much, and when. Do not induce vomiting unless explicitly instructed by a professional, as this can sometimes worsen the situation. Collect any remaining substance or packaging for identification.

3. Choking: Every Second Counts

Signs: Look for difficulty breathing, excessive pawing at the mouth, blue or purple tongue, panic, and distress.

Response: If your dog can still breathe, encourage them to cough up the object. For a completely obstructed airway, perform the Heimlich maneuver for dogs: For small dogs, hold them with their back against your chest and apply quick, upward thrusts to the abdomen just behind the rib cage. For larger dogs, place one hand on each side of the rib cage and apply quick, inward and upward thrusts. Once the object is dislodged, seek immediate veterinary care to check for any potential injuries.

4. Severe Bleeding: Control the Situation Quickly

Signs: Look for obvious wounds, blood-soaked fur, or continuous bleeding from any part of the body.

Response: Apply direct, firm pressure to the wound using a clean cloth or sterile gauze. If blood soaks through, add more layers without removing the original dressing. For limb injuries, elevate the limb above the heart if possible. If you suspect internal bleeding (swollen abdomen, pale gums, collapse), keep your dog calm and still. In all cases of severe bleeding, seek immediate veterinary care while continuing to apply pressure during transport.

Remember, while these immediate responses can be life-saving, they are not substitutes for professional veterinary care. Always follow up with your veterinarian after any health emergency, even if your dog appears to have recovered.

Lost Dog Protocol: When Your Best Friend Goes Missing

Taking preventive measures is crucial to ensure your dog's safety and increase the chances of a swift reunion if they ever go missing. Here are some essential steps to implement:

Invest in permanent identification:

- Have your dog microchipped by a veterinarian, ensuring the chip is registered with up-to-date contact information
- Outfit your dog with a sturdy collar featuring clearly legible ID tags containing your current phone number and address

Create a comprehensive digital and physical portfolio:

- Capture high-resolution, full-body photographs of your dog from various angles, including close-ups of any distinguishing features
- Maintain a detailed written description of your dog, including breed, size, color, and any unique markings or characteristics

Swift Action Plan: When Your Furry Friend Vanishes

In the unfortunate event that your dog goes missing, time is of the essence. Follow these steps immediately:

1. Conduct a thorough, systematic search of your immediate vicinity, including your home, yard, and surrounding neighborhood
2. Reach out to local animal shelters, veterinary clinics, and animal control agencies, providing them with your dog's description and your contact information
3. Launch a multi-faceted awareness campaign:
    - Design eye-catching flyers featuring a clear photo and essential details about your dog
    - Distribute these flyers throughout your neighborhood, local businesses, and community centers
    - Harness the power of social media by sharing your dog's information across various platforms, en-

couraging friends and followers to spread the word

4. Utilize specialized lost pet services and technologies:
    - Register your lost dog on dedicated platforms like PawBoost, which can amplify your search efforts
    - Leverage community-based apps such as Nextdoor to alert nearby residents and tap into local knowledge
    - Consider employing pet-finding services that use scent-tracking dogs or facial recognition technology to aid in the search

Technology in Emergencies: Modern Tools for Pet Safety

Harness the power of modern technology to enhance your dog's safety and well-being:

1. GPS tracking collars: These innovative devices offer real-time location tracking for dogs with a tendency to wander, providing peace of mind and facilitating quick recovery if your furry friend strays too far.
2. Smart pet camera systems: Install high-definition cameras with two-way audio capabilities to monitor and interact with your dog when you're away from home, ensuring their comfort and security.
3. Comprehensive pet health apps: Utilize applications like PetFirst Aid by the American Red Cross, which offer quick access to vital information, step-by-step guides for common emergencies, and the ability to locate nearby veterinary clinics in urgent situations.
4. Digital pet health management platforms: Take advantage of online portals that securely store and organize

your dog's medical records, vaccination history, and treatment plans, allowing for easy access and sharing with veterinarians or pet sitters as needed.

5. Smart feeding systems: Implement automated feeders with portion control and scheduling features to maintain your dog's dietary routine, even when you're not at home.

Special Considerations: Seniors and Special Needs Dogs

If your dog is a senior or has special needs, it's crucial to take extra precautions and make specific arrangements to ensure their safety and comfort during emergencies. Consider the following measures:

1. Enhance your emergency kit with specialized equipment: Include any mobility aids, such as ramps or slings, that your dog may require for safe and comfortable movement. Don't forget to pack extra padding or orthopedic bedding to provide proper support during extended periods away from home.
2. Create a comprehensive care instruction manual: Develop a detailed document outlining your dog's specific needs, including medication schedules, dietary requirements, and any unique routines or comfort measures. This information will be invaluable for potential caretakers who may need to assist your dog during an emergency.
3. Invest in appropriate transportation gear: Research and acquire a specially designed harness or carrier that accommodates your dog's physical limitations. Look for options that offer additional support, easy access, and comfort features tailored to senior or special needs dogs. This will make evacuations and veterinary visits much smoother

and less stressful for both you and your furry companion.

4. Establish a network of familiar caregivers: Identify and connect with friends, family members, or professional pet sitters who are willing and able to care for your senior or special needs dog in case of an emergency. Familiarize them with your dog's specific requirements and ensure they have access to your detailed care instructions.
5. Keep medical records easily accessible: Maintain an up-to-date file of your dog's medical history, including current medications, recent test results, and any ongoing treatments. Store this information in both physical and digital formats for quick retrieval during emergencies.

The Crucial Role of Support Networks in Dog Ownership

Navigating the challenges of dog ownership becomes significantly more manageable when you have a robust support system in place. By cultivating a network of resources and relationships, you can access valuable guidance, share experiences, and find comfort in knowing that you're not alone in your journey. Here are some key avenues to consider when building your support network:

- Engage with local or online dog owner communities:
  - Participate in breed-specific forums or general dog owner groups to exchange advice and experiences
  - Attend local meetups or dog park gatherings to connect with fellow dog owners in your area
- Establish a strong relationship with a trusted veterinarian:

    - Schedule regular check-ups to maintain open communication about your dog's health
    - Don't hesitate to reach out with questions or concerns between visits

- Collaborate with professional trainers or behaviorists:

    - Seek expert guidance for specific behavioral issues or training goals
    - Consider attending group classes to learn alongside other dog owners

- Foster connections with dog-loving friends and family members:

    - Share your experiences and seek advice from those who understand your bond with your dog
    - Organize dog-friendly gatherings to strengthen your support network

As you face new challenges and milestones in your dog ownership journey, don't hesitate to expand and nurture these connections. The collective wisdom and empathy of your support network can provide invaluable assistance, encouragement, and companionship along the way.

Challenges in dog ownership are not just obstacles to overcome; they're opportunities for growth – both for you and your dog. Each hurdle you navigate successfully deepens your understanding, strengthens your bond, and makes you a more confident, compassionate dog owner.

It's okay to struggle sometimes. Dog ownership isn't about perfection; it's about commitment, love, and the willingness to learn and adapt. Don't be afraid to seek help when you need it, celebrate small victories, and always keep your dog's well-being at the heart of your decisions.

As you face and overcome challenges together, you'll discover reserves of patience, creativity, and resilience you never knew you had. Here's to the challenges that make us better pet parents and the dogs who inspire us to rise to the occasion!

12. Dog Boarding

When circumstances require you to be away from your beloved canine companion, ensuring their comfort, safety, and emotional well-being naturally becomes your paramount concern. While the marketplace offers numerous professional boarding facilities as a potential solution, these shouldn't automatically be considered your primary option. Instead, let's carefully examine all available choices for your furry friend's care, beginning with the most beneficial arrangements and systematically working our way through various alternatives that might become necessary depending on your specific situation.

First Choice: Family and Friends

Why Family and Friends Are Best

Entrusting your dog's care to family and friends offers numerous advantages that make it the ideal choice for most pet owners. Your dog benefits from staying with people they already know and trust, which significantly reduces stress and anxiety during your absence. By maintaining their regular routine in a familiar environment - whether it's their own home or a well-known location - your pet can feel more secure and comfortable.

Taking a thoughtful, long-term approach is absolutely essential when establishing care arrangements with family and friends for your beloved pet. This process requires careful planning and dedication to ensure your dog develops genuine comfort and trust with potential caregivers. Surprising either your pet or your loved ones with unexpected care requests can create unnecessary stress and anxiety, potentially leading to unsuccessful care arrangements and strained relationships.

Instead, the most effective strategy is to systematically build familiarity through regular, planned interactions and visits to their homes. These consistent encounters allow both your dog and potential caregivers to naturally develop mutual understanding and comfort with each other's daily rhythms, individual preferences, and unique characteristics. During these visits, your dog can become accustomed to their feeding schedules, house rules, and living environment, while caregivers can learn about your pet's specific behavioural patterns, dietary needs, exercise requirements, and any special considerations or quirks that make your dog unique. This gradual, intentional approach helps establish a strong foundation of trust and understanding that will prove invaluable when actual care needs arise.

The benefit of having someone you trust board your pet is the one-on-one attention they receive ensures their individual needs are met, while regular updates keep you connected and informed about your pet's wellbeing. Additionally, while it's important to offer compensation, this option often proves more cost-effective than professional services, making it a practical choice for both you and your furry friend.

Making It Work with Family/Friends

Here's a comprehensive framework for working with family and friends when arranging dog care:

Essential Preparation Checklist:

Before leaving your dog with family or friends, ensure you provide all necessary materials and information:

- Detailed written instructions for your dog's care
- Complete veterinary contact information and medical history
- A list of emergency contacts
- Sufficient food and essential supplies
- Necessary access items like house keys and security codes

Showing Gratitude:

- Make sure to properly acknowledge their help:
- Provide appropriate compensation
- Offer to reciprocate their assistance when needed
- Express your sincere appreciation
- Consider giving a thoughtful gift

Communication Guidelines:

Establish clear expectations and protocols:

- Be specific about daily care routines
- Decide on the best way to stay in touch
- Create clear emergency procedures
- Clearly communicate any household rules or preferences

Second Choice: Professional Pet Sitters

Benefits of Pet Sitters

Professional pet sitters offer several significant advantages that make them an excellent choice for dog care. First and foremost, your pet can remain in their familiar home environment, which significantly reduces stress and anxiety during your absence. This arrangement allows your dog to maintain their regular daily routine, including familiar feeding times, walks, and rest periods. Pet sitters provide dedicated one-on-one attention, ensuring your dog receives personalized care tailored to their specific needs and preferences. Throughout your time away, you'll receive regular updates and communication about your pet's well-being, offering peace of mind. As an added benefit, having someone regularly visit your home provides additional security through consistent presence and activity at your property.

Finding a Reliable Pet Sitter

1. Get recommendations from:

    - Your veterinarian
    - Local pet owners
    - Pet supply stores
    - Online pet-sitting platforms

2. Essential Qualifications:

    - Experience with dogs
    - Pet first-aid certification
    - Insurance coverage
    - Background checks
    - References

Last Resort: Professional Boarding Facilities

When circumstances prevent you from arranging care with family, friends, or professional pet sitters, boarding facilities present themselves as a viable alternative for your pet's temporary accommodation. While this may not be your first preference, boarding facilities can still provide quality care when properly vetted and selected. To ensure you make an informed decision that best serves your pet's needs, let's explore the essential considerations for choosing the right boarding facility.

Evaluating a Boarding Facility

Physical Facility Assessment

- Cleanliness and sanitation protocols - Daily disinfection of all areas, proper waste disposal systems, regular deep cleaning schedules, and use of pet-safe cleaning products to prevent disease transmission
- Ventilation and temperature control - Well-maintained HVAC systems, proper air circulation to prevent airborne diseases, consistent comfortable temperature (typically 20-26°C), and humidity control to ensure pet comfort
- Secure fencing and gates - Double-gate entry systems, minimum 6-foot fence height, dig-proof barriers, properly maintained locks and latches, and regular security inspections
- Size of kennels/runs - Spacious individual kennels (minimum 4x6 feet for medium dogs), raised sleeping areas, proper drainage systems, and non-slip flooring for safety
- Exercise areas - Multiple secure outdoor spaces, separate areas for different sized dogs, weather-protected zones, proper drainage, and safe, durable play equipment
- Separation of dogs by size/temperament - Dedicated areas for small, medium, and large dogs, quiet spaces for nervous pets, and separate sections for senior or special needs dogs

Staff Qualifications

- Training and experience - Staff must have formal pet care certifications, minimum 2 years hands-on experience working with various dog breeds, and undergo regular training updates on animal behavior, first aid, and handling techniques

- Staff-to-dog ratio - Maintain maximum 1:5 staff-to-dog ratio to ensure adequate supervision and attention for each pet's needs
- Veterinary partnerships - Established relationships with local veterinary clinics for routine and emergency care, including 24/7 on-call veterinary support and regular health consultations
- Emergency protocols - Detailed written procedures for medical emergencies, natural disasters, and facility issues, with staff regularly trained in CPR and first aid for pets
- 24/7 supervision policy - Round-the-clock staffing with overnight monitoring, regular security checks, and video surveillance to ensure continuous pet safety and care

Daily Routine

- Exercise schedule - Multiple daily walks (typically 3-4 times) with dedicated outdoor time, structured play sessions, and appropriate rest periods between activities to prevent overexertion
- Feeding times - Regular meals served at consistent times (usually morning and evening) following each dog's specific dietary requirements and portion sizes, with fresh water available at all times
- Playtime opportunities - Supervised group play sessions with compatible dogs, individual enrichment activities, and mental stimulation through toys and games appropriate for each dog's energy level
- Cleaning schedule - Regular sanitation throughout the

day including immediate waste removal, thorough kennel cleaning twice daily, disinfection of common areas, and weekly deep cleaning of all facilities
- Medication administration if needed - Careful tracking and documentation of all medications, administered precisely at prescribed times by trained staff members following veterinary instructions

Health and Safety

- Vaccination requirements - Must show proof of current vaccinations including rabies, distemper, parvo, and bordetella (kennel cough). Records must be from a licensed veterinarian and dated within the last year. Some facilities may require additional vaccinations based on local regulations.
- Flea/tick prevention policies - Regular flea/tick treatment required and verified upon check-in. Facility should conduct routine checks and have protocols for isolation if parasites are detected. Documentation of recent preventative treatment typically required.
- Disease outbreak protocols - Clear procedures for isolating sick animals, sanitizing affected areas, and notifying pet owners. Should include specific steps for common conditions like kennel cough or gastrointestinal issues, with designated quarantine areas and enhanced cleaning procedures.
- Emergency procedures - Detailed written plans for medical emergencies, natural disasters, and facility issues. Staff should be trained in pet first aid and CPR. Clear evacuation routes and emergency transport arrangements must

be established.

- On-call veterinary support - 24/7 access to veterinary care through partnerships with local clinics. Should have established relationships with multiple vets and emergency animal hospitals, with clear procedures for emergency transport and treatment authorization.

Services and Amenities

- Individual attention options - One-on-one playtime sessions with staff members, customized exercise routines, and personalized attention to meet your dog's specific needs. Staff can provide extra cuddles, individual training reinforcement, or quiet time based on your pet's preferences.
- Group play sessions - Supervised socialization opportunities where dogs are carefully matched by size, temperament, and energy level. Sessions typically last 30-60 minutes and include structured activities, free play, and rest periods.
- Webcam access - Real-time video streaming service allowing you to check on your pet throughout the day through secure online portals. Many facilities offer mobile apps for convenient viewing and peace of mind.
- Additional services (grooming, training) - Optional services like baths, nail trims, brush-outs, and basic training reinforcement. Some facilities offer professional grooming services and certified trainers who can work with your dog during their stay.

While these standards may seem demanding, quality pet

boarding facilities should meet most, if not all, of these requirements. When entrusting your beloved pet to an unfamiliar environment, it's crucial to find a facility that satisfies as many criteria as possible. The best facilities not only meet these standards but also work diligently to maintain them. Though running a pet boarding center requires significant effort, many dedicated professionals excel at it and operate their facilities with the highest standards.

Red Flags to Watch out For

Having explored all the essential requirements in depth, let's examine some definite red flags that should prevent you from boarding your pets at a facility under any circumstances.

1. Reluctance to give tours - If a facility refuses to show you their entire premises during normal business hours or only allows restricted access to certain areas, this could indicate they're hiding poor conditions or questionable practices. A reputable facility should be proud to showcase their operations and transparent about all aspects of their service.
2. Unpleasant odors - While some animal-related smells are normal, strong, persistent odors often indicate inadequate cleaning protocols or poor ventilation. Quality facilities maintain rigorous cleaning schedules and proper air circulation systems to minimize unpleasant smells and maintain a healthy environment.
3. Unsanitary conditions - Look for signs of neglected cleaning such as accumulated waste, dirty water bowls, soiled bedding, or visible dirt and grime. Professional facilities should maintain spotless conditions with regular cleaning

throughout the day and thorough sanitization protocols.

4. Overcrowding - Too many dogs in a limited space can lead to stress, fights, and disease transmission. Each dog should have adequate personal space in their kennel and during group activities. Quality facilities strictly limit their capacity and maintain appropriate staff-to-dog ratios.
5. Unhappy or stressed dogs - Observe the boarding dogs' behavior. Excessive barking, cowering, aggression, or lethargy can indicate poor care or stressful conditions. Well-cared-for dogs should appear relaxed, engaged, and comfortable in their environment.
6. Evasive answers about procedures - Staff should be able to clearly explain their daily routines, emergency protocols, and handling procedures. Vague or inconsistent answers may indicate lack of proper training or established protocols.
7. Poor staff interaction with animals - Watch how staff members handle and communicate with the dogs. They should display patience, gentleness, and genuine affection. Rough handling, harsh voices, or indifference to the animals' needs are major warning signs.
8. Lack of proper licensing - All boarding facilities must have current licenses and permits as required by local regulations. Ask to see these documents - reputable facilities will readily provide proof of their legal compliance and certifications.
9. No emergency protocols - The facility should have detailed written procedures for medical emergencies, natural disasters, and other crisis situations. Staff should be able to explain these protocols and demonstrate knowl-

edge of emergency procedures.

10. Required vaccination records not checked - A quality facility will strictly enforce vaccination requirements and carefully review all health documentation before accepting any animals. Failure to verify health records puts all boarding pets at risk of disease transmission.

Preparing for Boarding

Health Requirements

- Updated vaccinations - Ensure all core vaccines (rabies, distemper, parvo) are current and documented. Many facilities require Bordetella (kennel cough) vaccination within the last 6 months.
- Current flea/tick prevention - Must have proof of recent flea and tick treatment, typically within the last 30 days. This protects all pets in the facility.
- Health certificate if required - Some facilities need a recent (within 10 days) certificate from your vet stating your dog is healthy and free from contagious diseases.
- Medication instructions - Provide detailed written instructions for any medications, including dosage, timing, and administration method. Include your vet's contact information.

What to Pack

- Regular food in portioned bags - Package each meal separately to maintain consistency and prevent digestive issues. Include feeding schedule and any special instructions.

- Favorite toys (limit to 2-3) - Choose durable, washable toys that provide comfort but won't cause possessiveness in group settings. Label each item with your dog's name.
- Familiar bedding - A blanket or bed that smells like home can help reduce anxiety. Ensure it's washable and clearly labeled.
- Detailed care instructions - Write down your dog's routine, preferences, commands used, and any behavioral quirks or special needs.
- Emergency contacts - Include your contact information, backup contact, veterinarian details, and any insurance information.
- Medication if needed - Pack extra doses in case of extended stay. Provide original containers with prescription labels.

Trial Run

- Schedule a short stay before longer trips - Book a one-night stay to assess how your dog adapts to the new environment and caregivers.
- Observe your dog's response - Pay attention to their behavior during drop-off and pick-up, appetite, energy levels, and overall demeanor after the trial stay.
- Evaluate facility's communication - Check how well they keep you informed, whether they follow your instructions, and their responsiveness to questions.
- Address any concerns early - Discuss any issues or adjustments needed based on the trial stay before booking longer periods.

Making the Transition Easier

Before You Leave

- Exercise your dog well before drop-off - Take your dog for a long walk or engage in vigorous play before heading to the boarding facility. This helps burn excess energy, reduces anxiety, and increases the likelihood they'll rest well during their first day at the facility.
- Maintain a calm demeanor during goodbye - Dogs are highly attuned to their owners' emotions. Stay relaxed and upbeat during drop-off, as your anxiety can transfer to your pet. Use a cheerful, normal tone of voice and maintain positive body language.
- Keep farewells brief and positive - Prolonged, emotional goodbyes can increase your dog's stress levels. Instead, give a quick pat, a happy "see you soon," and exit confidently. This helps your dog understand that the situation is normal and temporary.
- Leave something with your scent - Provide a recently worn (unwashed) t-shirt or small blanket that carries your familiar smell. This comfort item can help ease anxiety and provide reassurance during their stay. Make sure the item is something you won't miss if it gets damaged.

During the Stay

- Don't call to check on your dog - While it's tempting to call and ask about your pet, this can actually be counterproductive. Phone calls may cause staff to interrupt your dog's routine, and hearing your voice without seeing you could trigger anxiety or confusion in your pet. Instead, trust that no news is good news.

- Review updates/photos from the facility - Many modern boarding facilities offer photo updates or daily report cards through apps or email. These allow you to monitor your pet's activities and well-being without disrupting their stay. Set specific times to check these updates rather than constantly monitoring them.
- Trust the caregivers you've chosen - Remember that you selected this facility after careful research and verification. The staff are professionals who handle many dogs and know how to provide appropriate care. Your confidence in their abilities will help you relax and enjoy your time away.
- Have a backup plan in case of issues - While problems are rare, it's wise to have contingency plans. This might include having a trusted friend or family member on standby, knowing the location of nearby alternative facilities, or having funds set aside for unexpected veterinary care. Share these backup plans with the facility.

A Note on Separation Anxiety

Some dogs struggle more with separation than others. If your dog has separation anxiety:

- Work with a trainer before boarding becomes necessary - Start training sessions well in advance to help your dog build confidence and coping skills. A professional trainer can teach techniques like relaxation protocols, desensitization to separation, and positive associations with new environments. Regular training sessions over several weeks or months can significantly improve your dog's ability to handle time away from you.

- Consider anti-anxiety medications (consult your vet) - Schedule a consultation with your veterinarian to discuss medication options. They may recommend short-term anti-anxiety medications for boarding stays or longer-term treatments depending on your dog's specific needs. Your vet can evaluate your dog's health history, conduct necessary tests, and create a tailored medication plan with proper dosing instructions.
- Choose facilities experienced with anxious dogs - Look for boarding facilities that specifically advertise experience with anxious pets. These facilities should have quiet spaces, calming routines, and staff trained in recognizing and managing stress behaviors. Ask about their specific protocols for anxious dogs, including extra monitoring, specialized attention, and stress-reduction techniques.
- Prioritize in-home care options when possible - Arrange for a trusted pet sitter to stay at your home or have your dog stay at a familiar friend's house. This maintains your dog's routine and environment, minimizing stress triggers. In-home care allows for one-on-one attention, familiar surroundings, and continuation of normal daily activities that help reduce anxiety.

While boarding facilities serve an important purpose and can be the right choice in some situations, exploring options that keep your dog in a familiar environment with known caregivers should always be your first priority. Whatever option you choose, thorough research, careful preparation, and clear communication will help ensure your dog receives the best possible care during your absence.

Remember, every dog is different. What works for one might not work for another. Pay attention to your dog's personality and needs when making care decisions, and always have a backup plan ready. Your peace of mind and your dog's well-being are worth the extra effort in finding the right care solution.

13. Traveling With Your Dog

Ah, the joys of traveling with your furry best friend! If you're planning to explore the diverse landscapes of India with your canine companion, you're in for a treat. But before you pack those chew toys and hit the road, let's dive into the nitty-gritty of making your adventure as smooth as a Labrador's coat.

General Preparation for All Types of Travel

Before embarking on your adventure with your furry companion, it's crucial to cover some universal preparations that will ensure a smooth and enjoyable journey, regardless of your chosen mode of travel. Let's delve into these essential steps:

1. **Veterinary Check-up**: Schedule a comprehensive examination with your veterinarian to ensure your dog is in optimal health for travel. This visit should include updating any necessary vaccinations and obtaining a health certificate, which may be required for certain types of travel or destinations.

2. **Proper Identification**: Equip your dog with a sturdy collar bearing an ID tag that displays your current contact information. For added security, consider microchipping your pet if you haven't already done so. This permanent form of identification can be a lifesaver if your dog becomes separated from you during your travels.
3. **Travel Acclimatization**: Gradually familiarize your dog with their travel carrier or harness well in advance of your trip. This process may involve short practice sessions where you introduce your pet to the carrier or harness, gradually increasing the duration of wear or confinement. This preparation can significantly reduce stress and anxiety during the actual journey.
4. **Essential Packing List**: Assemble a comprehensive kit of travel essentials for your canine companion, including:

    - Ample supply of your dog's regular food and treats
    - Portable food and water bowls for convenient feeding on-the-go
    - Sufficient water to keep your pet hydrated throughout the journey
    - Any necessary medications, along with detailed dosage instructions
    - Multiple leashes and collars (in case of loss or damage)
    - An abundance of waste bags for responsible clean-up
    - Your dog's favorite toys and comfort items to provide familiarity in new environments
    - Comfortable bedding to ensure restful sleep during your travels
    - A well-stocked pet first-aid kit for any unforeseen

emergencies

- Recent photographs of your dog for identification purposes if needed

5. **Thorough Research**: Conduct extensive research on pet-friendly accommodations, attractions, and amenities at your destination. This includes identifying nearby veterinary clinics, dog parks, and pet supply stores. Additionally, familiarize yourself with local leash laws and any breed-specific regulations that may affect your travel plans.
6. **Documentation Preparation**: Gather and organize all necessary documentation for your pet, including vaccination records, health certificates, and any required travel permits. Make multiple copies of these documents and store them in easily accessible locations.

Thorough planning is the key to transforming potential travel challenges into opportunities for bonding and creating lasting memories with your four-legged friend.

Traveling by Car

Car travel offers unparalleled flexibility for pet owners, allowing you to create a tailored journey for both you and your furry companion. Let's explore how to ensure a safe, comfortable, and enjoyable road trip experience:

Prioritizing Safety on the Road

- Secure your dog with a well-ventilated, crash-tested crate or a specially designed dog seat belt harness to prevent injury during sudden stops or accidents

- If your dog is prone to motion sickness, consider these steps:

  - Consult your veterinarian about anti-nausea medications suitable for dogs
  - Feed your dog a light meal 3-4 hours before travel, avoiding food right before the trip
  - Ensure proper ventilation in the car to reduce nausea
  - Take frequent breaks to allow your dog to walk and get fresh air
  - Use calming aids like pheromone sprays or anxiety wraps if stress contributes to the sickness

- Keep your canine companion in the back seat or cargo area to protect them from airbag deployment and reduce driver distraction

- Resist the temptation to let your dog hang out the window, as this can lead to eye injuries from debris or worse if they attempt to jump out
- Never leave your dog unattended in a parked car, as temperatures can quickly reach dangerous levels, even on seemingly mild days

Mapping Out a Dog-Friendly Route

- Schedule regular pit stops every 2-3 hours to allow your dog to stretch, relieve themselves, and burn off some energy
- Research and plan your route to include dog-friendly rest areas, parks, or pet-welcoming establishments along the way
- Consider using pet-friendly travel apps to easily locate suitable stopping points during your journey

Enhancing Comfort for the Long Haul

- Prepare your dog for extended car trips by gradually increasing the duration of rides in the weeks leading up to your big adventure
- Create a cozy haven in the car by bringing your dog's favorite bedding, blankets, or travel bed to provide a sense of familiarity and security
- Pack comfort items like their preferred toys or a shirt with your scent to help ease any travel anxiety
- If your dog is prone to motion sickness, consult your veterinarian about appropriate anti-nausea medications or

natural remedies to ensure a more pleasant journey

Navigating Legal and Practical Considerations

- Familiarize yourself with leash laws, pet regulations, and dog-friendly areas in the regions you'll be passing through to avoid any legal complications
- Carry up-to-date copies of your dog's vaccination records and any necessary health certificates, especially if crossing state or international borders
- Consider investing in pet insurance that covers travel-related incidents for added peace of mind during your road trip

Traveling by Train

Indian Railways has its own set of rules you need to be mindful of when traveling with your pooch.

- Indian Railways transports millions of passengers daily. The trains are often crowded, and securing a confirmed ticket is rarely guaranteed, especially for higher classes. To travel with your pets on the train, you must book First Class or 1A Class tickets. Be aware that there are only one or two 1A coaches per train, limiting ticket availability.
- Not every train has a first-class coach. If your chosen route doesn't offer a train with a First Class Coach, you unfortunately can't travel with your dogs on that train. Don't worry, though—we'll discuss an alternative option later.
- Book as early as possible. Aim to secure your tickets be-

tween a month and 20 days before your journey to increase your chances of confirmation. Remember, first-class tickets aren't available under the Tatkal scheme, so advance booking is essential.

- When traveling with dogs in first class, you'll need either a **coupe** (a two-person cabin) or a **cabin** (4 seats), and everyone in the cabin must be part of your group. For context, each 1A coach typically has only 3-4 coupes, with the rest being cabins. To secure a coupe, you need to book at least two tickets. When booking on IRCTC, select the "Coupe" option under preferences.
- If you're traveling with 3 or 4 people, you'll likely be assigned a cabin by default. However, if you book only one ticket, there's no guarantee of getting a coupe. In most cases, you'll be allocated a cabin where you won't be allowed to bring your pet unless all other passengers in the cabin are part of your group.

Documentation

To travel with your pet by train, you'll need the following documents:

- A fit-to-travel certificate: Visit the vet 2-3 days before your journey. This health certificate is valid for only 24-48 hours before your train's departure.
- Vaccination history and treatment records: The standard booklet is sufficient, but it's wise to keep a couple of extra copies on hand.
- Request for a coupe: This crucial step helps secure a private compartment for you and your dog. Here's what you need to do:

- Write a letter detailing your travel plans with your pet and request a coupe.
- Include copies of Aadhaar cards for all travelers, your ticket with PNR, and all necessary travel details.
- Two days before your journey, submit these documents in a sealed envelope to the "Emergency Quota" department at the reservation office of your train's originating station.
- Note: Even if you've requested a coupe while booking, it's not guaranteed. High-ranking officials and ministers take precedence.

Dog ticket: Your furry friend needs their own "luggage ticket." Here's how to get one:

- Visit the station at least 4 hours before departure.
- Bring copies of your Aadhaar cards, your dog's vaccination records, and health certificate.
- Head to the 'Luggage booking' room with your dog.
- Present your dog and all documents for processing.
- Fees are typically Rs. 80 per kilo, but sometimes a flat rate of Rs. 1100 per dog is charged.
- Note: As of now, you must book these tickets in person, but online booking may soon be available according to recent reports in the media.

During the travel

You've secured your tickets, a coupe, and luggage tickets. Now, keep everything organized and ensure you have all necessities for a comfortable journey. Here are some best practices to follow once you've boarded the train with your dogs:

- Spread loose newspapers on the floor to protect against "accidents"—some dogs may experience travel sickness.
- Familiarize yourself with all station stops well in advance.
- Use a poop scooper to clean up after your dogs and newspaper to absorb urine. Never leave waste on the station platform.
- Keep your dogs leashed when outside your coupe to avoid inconveniencing other travelers. Remember, traveling with pets on public transport is a privilege. To foster kindness towards dogs and their caregivers, the responsibility of being a considerate pet parent rests on you.

The Guard Van

In the worst-case scenario where you don't get assigned a coupe and fellow travelers in a cabin are uncomfortable with a pet, you'll need to place your dog in the guard van. The dog is "booked as luggage in the luggage-cum-Brake Van under the Train Manager's (Guard's) supervision."

- On the train, your furry friend will be placed in a 'dog box'—a large cage in the luggage-cum-brake-van, which is essentially a small compartment containing only the dog box and a guard. While you're not allowed to sit in the Brake Van, you can easily "visit" your pet since it's usually located next to the "General" coach.
- This option lets you book any class of ticket for yourself, just like a regular passenger. You're even free to travel in General class if you prefer.
- You'll only be allowed to reclaim your dog at the destination station as per your ticket—not before or after.

This option is viable if your dog can handle being confined to a cage for the entire train journey. During longer stops, you might be allowed to walk your dog if you ask the van guard nicely. Keep in mind that not all trains have an animal carrier cage. Even when they do, availability isn't guaranteed as there's typically only one dog box per train, offered on a first-come, first-served basis.

Amlan had an unforgettable experience traveling with his pet Oreo. When visiting family in Bhubaneswar, they couldn't arrange boarding for Oreo and decided to take him along. After thorough research—reading articles online and consulting experienced pet travelers—Amlan felt prepared. The outbound journey from Bangalore was delightful, with a first-class coupe allotted to them. Oreo traveled comfortably with his favorite humans, without disturbing any fellow passengers or getting disturbed by them.

The return journey to Bangalore, however, proved challenging. Amlan had overlooked a crucial detail about traveling with dogs on Indian trains: when booking a first-class ticket, one must request a coupe allotment and obtain a dog ticket from the train's point of origin—in this case, Kolkata. Upon reaching Bhubaneswar station on departure day, officials informed him of this requirement. But since the train had already departed from Kolkata hours earlier, nothing could be done. The officials explained that Amlan would be assigned to a four-person cabin, and if his co-passengers objected to Oreo's presence, the dog would have to travel in the guard van.

As Amlan and his wife contemplated alternatives, they fortunately met another passenger traveling with her dog. Through a stroke of luck, this lady had a coupe allotment but knew a couple who had boarded in Kolkata and wanted her company in their cabin. Amlan arranged to exchange accommodations with her, ensuring a comfortable journey with Oreo. While this situation worked out well for Amlan, many pet parents likely face similar challenges with travel restrictions. It's essential to verify the latest rules and regulations when planning to travel with your dog on Indian trains.

Traveling by Air

Air travel with pets demands the most preparation and often comes with the strictest regulations.

While the rules for domestic pet travel via flights aren't overly complex, they're non-negotiable. Failing to meet any requirement can result in your pet being denied boarding. Currently, only Air India and Akasa Air allow pets on their flights.

Here are the key guidelines for pet travel in India:

Size of Pet Carrier

For in-cabin travel, your pet's soft carrier must not exceed 18" x 18" x 12" (Length x Width x Height), with a maximum weight of 5 kg.

Larger pets must travel in the cargo hold in an IATA-approved fibre pet crate. The crate should be labeled with your pet's name and include a moisture-absorbent mat.

Pet Travel Criteria

Your pet must be at least eight weeks old to travel. Pregnant pets are not allowed to fly.

Required documentation includes your pet's health certificate, vaccination record, and any additional certificates as applicable.

While most pets can fly, some restrictions apply. For example, brachycephalic (snub-nosed) breeds of dogs and cats may face difficulties due to their physiology affecting breathing and temperature regulation. Always check with your airline about your specific pet before booking.

As the pet owner, you're responsible for complying with all government rules and regulations, including health and safety requirements.

Before flying, you must sign an indemnification form, assuming all risks of injury, sickness, or death of your pet during travel.

Pet travel incurs additional charges and isn't covered under free baggage allowance. For domestic flights in India, normal excess baggage charges apply, based on the combined weight of the container, pet, and food inside the crate.

Before You Book

- Check airline pet policies; they vary significantly between carriers
- Be aware of breed restrictions

Preparing for the Flight

- Invest in a high-quality, airline-approved pet carrier that provides ample space for your dog to comfortably stand, turn around, and lie down. Ensure the carrier meets all airline size and material requirements to avoid any last-minute issues at the airport.
- Begin the acclimation process well in advance of your flight date. Gradually introduce your dog to the carrier through positive reinforcement techniques, such as placing treats inside and rewarding calm behavior. Practice short car rides with the carrier to simulate travel conditions and help your dog associate it with positive experiences.
- Schedule a comprehensive veterinary check-up within 10 days of your departure date. This visit should include obtaining all necessary health certificates, updating vaccinations, and discussing any potential travel-related health concerns specific to your dog's breed or individual needs. Your vet can also provide advice on managing travel anxiety if needed.

- Carefully evaluate your dog's temperament and ability to handle the stress of air travel. Consider factors such as your dog's age, health status, and previous experiences with travel or unfamiliar environments. For some pets, alternative travel arrangements or leaving them with a trusted caregiver might be a more suitable option to ensure their well-being.

At the Airport

- Arrive at the airport well in advance of your scheduled departure time to allow for thorough check-in procedures and any unexpected delays. This extra time will help reduce stress for both you and your furry companion.
- Before entering the airport, take your dog for a leisurely walk or engage in some light exercise. This will help burn off excess energy and potentially reduce anxiety during the flight. It's also an excellent opportunity for a bathroom break.
- Familiarize yourself with the airport's pet security screening protocols. Be prepared to remove your dog from its carrier and walk through metal detectors together. Some airports may require additional screening measures, so stay calm and patient throughout the process to keep your pet at ease.
- Pack a small "pet travel kit" in your carry-on, including items like a collapsible water bowl, a few favorite toys, and any necessary medications. This kit can be invaluable for keeping your dog comfortable during unexpected delays or layovers.

During the Flight

- If your dog is traveling in the cabin, it's crucial to keep them inside their carrier throughout the flight. Removing your pet from the carrier can pose significant safety risks, not only for your dog but also for other passengers and flight crew. The confined space of an aircraft cabin is not suitable for pets to roam freely, and unexpected turbulence could lead to injury.
- For dogs traveling in the cargo hold, proper identification is paramount. Ensure that the carrier is clearly and securely labeled with your full name, contact information, and destination address. It's also wise to include a backup contact, such as a family member or your veterinarian, in case you're unreachable upon arrival.
- To minimize the risk of motion sickness and potential discomfort during the flight, it's advisable to withhold food from your dog for approximately 4-6 hours before departure. This precaution can help prevent nausea and reduce the likelihood of in-flight accidents. However, make sure to offer small amounts of water to keep your pet hydrated, especially for longer journeys.

International Travel

Traveling internationally with your pet involves navigating varying rules and regulations across countries. Some island nations, such as Australia and New Zealand, prohibit pet travel entirely, so thorough research is crucial before planning your trip.

- Research pet import regulations for your destination country well in advance

- Many countries require specific vaccinations, microchipping, and sometimes quarantine
- Obtain all necessary documentation, which may include:
    * Rabies vaccination certificate
    * International health certificate
    * Blood titer test (to assess your dog's immune system strength). Note that many countries don't accept blood titer tests conducted in India. You may need to send a blood sample to countries like the UK for testing, with results delivered via email.
    * Import permits as required

Before international travel with your pet, you'll need to complete multiple rounds of documentation and obtain approval from the cargo office regarding your travel, typically one day before your flight. It's advisable to consult pet relocation agencies, as they're well-versed in the intricacies and last-minute rule changes, ensuring a smooth travel experience.

While traveling with your pet requires extra planning and preparation, the joy of having your furry best friend by your side as you explore new places is unmatched. Every dog is different. Some may take to travel like a duck to water, while others might find it stressful. Always prioritize your dog's comfort and well-being, and be prepared to adjust your plans if needed.

So, are you ready to embark on your pawsome adventure? The world awaits you and your four-legged explorer!

14. Living With An Ageing Dog

Just as the autumn leaves bring a new beauty to the landscape, your dog's senior years can be a special time filled with deep bonds and gentle moments. As your furry friend enters their golden years, you'll notice changes – some subtle, others more pronounced. Understanding these changes is key to providing the best care and ensuring your senior dog's twilight years are comfortable, dignified, and filled with joy.

When is a Dog Considered "Senior"?

The transition into seniority is a gradual process that varies significantly depending on the breed and size of your canine companion:

- Small breeds: These pint-sized pooches typically enter their golden years around 10-12 years of age. Their longer life expectancy means they enjoy an extended adulthood before showing signs of seniority.
- Medium breeds: For our middle-of-the-pack friends, the

senior years often begin somewhere between 8-10 years. This transition period can vary widely depending on factors such as genetics, diet, and overall health.

- Large and giant breeds: Our gentle giants tend to age more rapidly, often considered seniors as early as 6-8 years. Their accelerated ageing process means they require attentive care and regular check-ups from a younger age.

It's crucial to remember that these age ranges are general guidelines and not set-in-stone rules. Each dog is a unique individual, and factors such as genetics, environment, diet, and overall health play significant roles in determining when your furry friend truly enters their senior years. Some dogs may show signs of ageing earlier, while others remain spry and youthful well into their later years.

Observing your dog's behaviour, energy levels, and any physical changes is often a more accurate indicator of their progression into seniority than their chronological age alone. Regular veterinary check-ups become increasingly important as your dog approaches and enters these milestone years, allowing for early detection and management of age-related changes or health concerns.

Physical Changes: The Visible Signs of Ageing

1. Graying Hair

As your canine companion ages, you may notice a gradual transformation in their coat color. This graying process, often referred to as "frosting," typically begins around the muzzle and eyebrows, giving your dog a distinguished and wise appearance.

This natural occurrence is akin to humans getting gray hair and is one of the most visible signs that your furry friend is entering their golden years.

2. Changes in Mobility

- Increased stiffness, particularly noticeable after periods of rest or upon waking
- Hesitation or difficulty when navigating stairs, jumping onto furniture, or getting in and out of vehicles
- A gradual decrease in endurance, leading to a preference for shorter walks and play sessions
- Potential development of a slight limp or favoring of certain limbs

3. Changes in Body Composition

- Gradual loss of muscle mass, particularly noticeable in the hind legs and along the spine
- Potential weight fluctuations: some seniors may gain weight due to decreased activity, while others might lose weight due to changes in metabolism or appetite
- Changes in body shape, such as a more pronounced spine or hip bones

4. Sensory Changes

- Development of a bluish haze in the eyes, known as lenticular sclerosis, which is a normal age-related change different from cataracts
- Gradual hearing loss, which may manifest as decreased responsiveness to verbal commands or environmental sounds
- Reduced sense of smell, potentially affecting appetite or

interest in exploring during walks

- Potential changes in night vision, leading to increased hesitation in dimly lit areas

5. Skin and Coat Changes

- Thinning of the coat, which may become more pronounced in certain areas
- Increased dryness or flakiness of the skin, potentially requiring additional grooming attention
- Development of various lumps, bumps, or skin tags (always consult with your veterinarian for proper evaluation)
- Potential changes in coat texture, such as increased coarseness or a softer, more downy feel

Behavioural Changes: The Subtle Shifts

1. Sleep Patterns

As dogs enter their senior years, their sleep patterns often undergo noticeable changes. These alterations can be attributed to various factors, including physical discomfort, cognitive changes, and shifts in their circadian rhythm.

- Increased daytime napping: Senior dogs may spend more time sleeping during daylight hours, often in shorter but more frequent naps.
- Nighttime restlessness: Many older dogs experience disrupted sleep at night, which can manifest as pacing, whining, or difficulty settling down.
- Changes in preferred sleeping locations: Your senior dog

may seek out new sleeping spots that offer more comfort or security.

2. Activity Level

The gradual decline in energy levels is a common aspect of canine ageing, impacting various aspects of your dog's daily routine:

- Reduced enthusiasm for previously enjoyed activities: Your once-energetic companion may show less interest in long walks or vigorous play sessions.
- Increased periods of rest: Senior dogs often require more downtime to recuperate between activities.
- Preference for gentler forms of exercise: Your ageing pet may gravitate towards less strenuous activities, such as shorter walks or calm indoor games.

3. Cognitive Changes

Cognitive Dysfunction Syndrome (CDS) can affect some senior dogs, leading to behavioural changes that may be subtle at first but become more pronounced over time:

- Disorientation or confusion: Your dog may appear lost in familiar surroundings or have difficulty navigating around furniture.
- Alterations in social interactions: Changes in how your dog engages with family members or other pets can be a sign of cognitive decline.
- Lapses in house training: Senior dogs may experience accidents indoors, even if they've been well-trained for years.
- Memory issues: Your dog might forget learned commands or routines they once performed effortlessly.

4. Emotional Changes

The emotional landscape of a senior dog can shift, often requiring adjustments in how you interact with and care for your ageing companion:

- Increased dependence or anxiety: Your dog may seek more attention or become distressed when left alone.
- Changes in tolerance levels: Some seniors may become more easily irritated or less patient with handling of certain situations.
- Shifts in affection patterns: Your dog might seek out more cuddle time or, conversely, prefer more solitude.
- Sensitivity to environmental changes: Older dogs often become more reactive to alterations in their routine or surroundings.

Aditya brought home a three-month-old beagle puppy and named him Casper. Like most beagles, Casper was inquisitive, energetic, and loud. Thankfully, Aditya's apartment complex was pet-friendly, and Casper quickly became everyone's favorite. He would seek out children playing in the apartment, running and playing with them to his heart's content. Casper was quite the mischief-maker too. He'd seize any opportunity to escape through Aditya's door and bound up and down the stairs, chasing after pigeons and stray cats—a delightful sight to behold.

Over the years, Casper has mellowed considerably. Now at nine years old, while not as mischievous or energetic, he remains just as affectionate and playful—only his approach has changed. These days, he takes shorter walks and isn't as keen on stairs. Rather than running around with children, he prefers sitting in the society's dog park, though he still howls when children pass by without stopping to say hello or give him a loving pat. Full credit to Aditya—while Casper may have aged, his spirit remains as bright as ever. I often share his story with pet parents seeking guidance on navigating their dogs' senior years.

Nutrition for the Senior Dog: Fuelling the Ageing Body

Just as humans require dietary adjustments as they age - with increased needs for certain nutrients and decreased caloric requirements - our canine companions also experience significant changes in their nutritional needs. As your dog advances in years, their nutritional requirements undergo important shifts to support their ageing body and maintain optimal health:

- Caloric Adjustment: With a natural decrease in activity levels, senior dogs often require fewer calories to maintain a healthy weight. However, it's crucial to balance calorie reduction with adequate nutrition to prevent muscle loss.
- Protein Prioritization: High-quality, easily digestible protein becomes increasingly important to preserve muscle mass and support immune function. Look for senior dog foods with premium protein sources listed as primary ingredients.
- Joint Support: Supplements such as glucosamine, chondroitin, and omega-3 fatty acids can play a vital role in maintaining joint health and mobility. These supplements may be incorporated into specially formulated senior dog foods or administered separately under veterinary guidance.
- Hydration Emphasis: Proper hydration becomes even more critical for senior dogs, as they may be more prone to kidney issues or have a decreased thirst drive. Ensure

constant access to fresh water and consider incorporating moisture-rich foods into their diet.

- Digestive Care: Many senior dogs benefit from added fiber to support digestive health and maintain regular bowel movements. Probiotics may also be beneficial for maintaining a healthy gut microbiome.

Given the unique needs of each ageing dog, it's essential to consult with your veterinarian to develop a tailored nutritional plan. They can recommend specific diets, supplements, or feeding strategies based on your senior dog's health status, breed, and individual requirements. Regular reassessment of your dog's nutritional needs is crucial as they continue to age and their health status evolves.

Exercise and Mental Stimulation: Keeping Body and Mind Active

While your senior dog may experience a natural decrease in energy levels, maintaining an active lifestyle remains crucial for their physical and mental well-being. Adapting their exercise routine to suit their changing needs can help keep them healthy and engaged:

- Implement shorter, more frequent walks throughout the day to accommodate reduced stamina while still providing regular physical activity
- Introduce low-impact exercises such as swimming or gentle hydrotherapy, which can be particularly beneficial for dogs with joint issues or arthritis
- Engage in gentle play sessions that cater to your dog's current abilities, focusing on quality interaction rather than

intense physical exertion

- Prioritize mental stimulation through interactive food puzzles, scent work activities, or teaching new, easy-to-learn tricks that challenge their cognitive abilities without overwhelming them
- Consider incorporating mild strength-building exercises, such as walking on different textures or navigating low obstacles, to help maintain muscle tone

It's essential to always let your senior dog set the pace during any activity. Be vigilant in observing their body language and behavior for signs of fatigue, discomfort, or overexertion. Remember that consistency is key – regular, moderate activity is often more beneficial than sporadic, intense sessions. Consult with your veterinarian to develop an exercise plan tailored to your senior dog's specific health needs and limitations.

The Importance of Comfort: Creating a Senior-Friendly Environment

Creating a senior-friendly environment through thoughtful modifications can significantly enhance your ageing dog's comfort and quality of life. Consider implementing these beneficial changes:

- Invest in supportive orthopedic beds to alleviate pressure on arthritic joints and promote restful sleep
- Install non-slip mats or rugs on slippery surfaces to prevent falls and increase your dog's confidence while moving around
- Utilize raised food and water bowls to reduce strain on your senior dog's neck and back during mealtimes

- Introduce ramps or steps for easier access to furniture, beds, or vehicles, preserving your dog's independence and mobility
- Establish and maintain a consistent, low-stress daily routine to provide a sense of security and reduce anxiety in your ageing companion

By implementing these small yet impactful changes, you can create a more comfortable and navigable environment that caters to your senior dog's evolving needs, promoting their overall well-being and happiness in their golden years.

Health Concerns in Senior Dogs

As our canine companions enter their golden years, their

health needs evolve. Proactive, informed care becomes crucial in ensuring our senior dogs maintain the best possible quality of life.

Regular Veterinary Check-ups

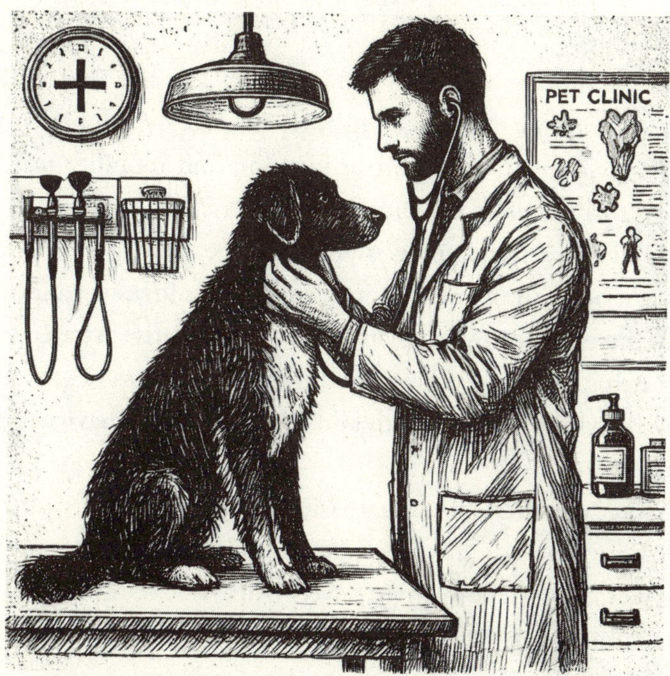

For senior dogs, veterinarians typically recommend bi-annual check-ups to ensure optimal health and early detection of age-related issues. These comprehensive examinations are crucial for maintaining your ageing companion's well-being and quality of life. During these visits, your veterinarian will conduct a thorough assessment that includes:

1. A detailed physical examination, evaluating every aspect of your dog's health from nose to tail
2. Comprehensive blood work to assess organ function, including liver and kidney panels, complete blood count,

and thyroid hormone levels

3. Urinalysis to check for signs of urinary tract infections, diabetes, or kidney disease
4. Blood pressure measurement to monitor cardiovascular health and detect hypertension, a common issue in older dogs
5. A thorough dental evaluation to identify and address periodontal disease, which can impact overall health
6. Assessment of cognitive function and mobility to catch early signs of dementia or arthritis

By identifying potential issues in their early stages, veterinarians can often implement more effective, less invasive, and more cost-efficient treatment plans. This preventative strategy not only helps manage existing conditions but also works to maintain your dog's overall health and comfort as they navigate their golden years.

Moreover, these bi-annual visits provide an excellent opportunity for you to discuss any changes you've noticed in your dog's behavior, appetite, or activity levels with your veterinarian. This open communication ensures that your furry friend receives personalized care tailored to their specific needs as they age.

Common Health Issues in Senior Dogs

1. Arthritis and Joint Problems

As dogs age, their joints may become less flexible and more prone to inflammation, leading to arthritis. This common condition can significantly impact a senior dog's quality of life if left unmanaged.

Signs:

- Morning stiffness or difficulty rising after prolonged periods of rest

- Hesitation or reluctance when climbing stairs, jumping onto furniture, or getting into vehicles
- Visible limping or favoring certain limbs during movement
- Decreased interest in physical activities they once enjoyed
- Licking or chewing at specific joints

Management:

- Implement a comprehensive weight management plan to reduce excess stress on joints
- Engage in low-impact, gentle exercise routines tailored to your dog's abilities, such as swimming or short, frequent walks
- Incorporate joint-supporting supplements like glucosamine, chondroitin, and omega-3 fatty acids into their diet
- Administer veterinarian-prescribed pain management medications to alleviate discomfort and improve mobility
- Explore alternative therapies such as acupuncture, physical therapy, or therapeutic massage to complement traditional treatments
- Create a comfortable living environment with orthopedic bedding and easy access to favorite resting spots
- Consider using ramps or steps to help your dog navigate furniture or vehicles more easily

2. Dental Disease: A Common Concern in Senior Canines

Dental disease, if left unchecked, can lead to serious health issues beyond just the mouth. Understanding the signs and implementing proper management strategies is crucial for maintaining your senior dog's overall well-being.

Signs of Dental Disease:

- Persistent bad breath (halitosis) that goes beyond normal "dog breath"
- Visible tartar buildup on teeth, often appearing as yellowish-brown deposits
- Redness, swelling, or bleeding of the gums, particularly when eating or playing with toys
- Difficulty eating, especially when attempting to chew hard foods
- Loose, discolored, or missing teeth
- Pawing at the mouth or face more frequently than usual
- Changes in behavior, such as increased irritability due to oral discomfort

Management:

- Schedule regular dental check-ups and professional cleanings with your veterinarian
- Implement a daily oral care routine, including gentle tooth brushing with dog-specific toothpaste or using dental wipes
- Provide dental chews, toys, or treats specifically designed to promote oral health and reduce tartar buildup
- Consider water additives or oral gels that help maintain dental hygiene between cleanings
- Explore diet options that support dental health, such as specially formulated dental kibble
- Be vigilant about checking your dog's mouth regularly for any changes or abnormalities

3. Cardiovascular Health in Senior Dogs

As dogs age, their heart health becomes increasingly important. Understanding the signs of heart disease and implementing proper management strategies can significantly improve your senior dog's quality of life.

Signs of Potential Heart Issues:

- Persistent coughing, particularly during the night or after physical activity
- Noticeable decrease in stamina during walks or play sessions
- Labored or rapid breathing, even when at rest
- Reluctance to engage in previously enjoyed activities
- Swelling in the abdomen (ascites) or limbs

Management:

- Adhere strictly to medication regimens prescribed by your veterinarian, which may include drugs to support heart function or manage fluid retention
- Implement dietary changes as recommended, often involving reduced sodium intake and increased omega-3 fatty acids
- Engage in gentle, consistent exercise routines tailored to your dog's current capabilities, always monitoring for signs of fatigue
- Schedule regular veterinary check-ups to monitor heart function and adjust treatment as necessary
- Consider complementary therapies such as acupuncture or massage, under veterinary guidance, to support overall well-being

4. Kidney Disease: A Common Concern in Ageing Canines

Kidney disease is a prevalent issue in senior dogs, often developing gradually over time. Understanding the signs and implementing proper management strategies is crucial for maintaining your ageing companion's quality of life and slowing the progression of the disease.

Signs of Kidney Disease:

- Noticeable increase in water consumption and urination frequency
- Gradual or sudden weight loss, often accompanied by muscle wasting
- Diminished appetite or complete loss of interest in food
- Lethargy and decreased interest in usual activities
- Vomiting or diarrhea, which may occur intermittently
- Bad breath with a distinctly urine-like odor

Management:

- Implementation of a specialized renal diet, formulated to reduce stress on the kidneys while providing essential nutrients
- Ensuring constant access to fresh, clean water to maintain proper hydration and support kidney function
- Administration of veterinarian-prescribed medications to manage symptoms, control blood pressure, and slow disease progression
- Regular blood work and urinalysis to monitor kidney function and adjust treatment as necessary
- Consideration of complementary therapies such as acupuncture or herbal supplements, under veterinary guidance
- Maintaining a stress-free environment to support overall well-being and reduce strain on the kidneys

5. Cognitive Dysfunction Syndrome (CDS): Understanding and Managing Canine Dementia

Cognitive Dysfunction Syndrome, often referred to as canine

dementia, is a complex neurological condition that affects many senior dogs. As our furry companions age, their cognitive abilities may decline, leading to a range of behavioral and functional changes. Recognizing the signs early and implementing appropriate management strategies can significantly improve the quality of life for dogs experiencing CDS.

Signs of CDS:

- Disorientation or confusion in familiar environments
- Altered sleep-wake cycles, often leading to nighttime restlessness and daytime lethargy
- Lapses in house training, even in well-trained dogs
- Changes in social interactions with family members or other pets
- Decreased responsiveness to commands or familiar cues
- Anxiety or restlessness, particularly in new situations

Management:

- Establishing and maintaining a consistent daily routine to reduce confusion and anxiety
- Providing mental stimulation through interactive puzzles, gentle play sessions, and new but manageable experiences
- Exploring medication options with your veterinarian to manage symptoms and slow progression
- Incorporating dietary supplements rich in antioxidants and omega-3 fatty acids to support brain health
- Creating a safe, comfortable environment with nightlights and easily accessible resources
- Engaging in regular, gentle exercise to promote physical and mental well-being
- Maintaining open communication with your veterinarian to adjust the care plan as needed

6. Cancer: A Complex Challenge in Senior Dogs

Cancer is a significant concern for ageing canines, manifesting in various forms and locations throughout the body. While the signs can be diverse and sometimes subtle, vigilance and regular veterinary care are crucial for early detection and management.

Potential Indicators of Canine Cancer:

- Presence of unusual growths, lumps, or swellings that persist or change over time
- Unexplained and persistent weight loss, despite maintaining normal eating habits
- Noticeable shifts in appetite, ranging from increased hunger to complete loss of interest in food
- Marked changes in energy levels, including lethargy or uncharacteristic fatigue
- Difficulty with bodily functions such as breathing, urinating, or defecating
- Non-healing wounds or sores that persist despite appropriate care

Management:

- Prioritize early detection through diligent at-home monitoring and scheduled veterinary check-ups
- Collaborate with your veterinarian to explore appropriate diagnostic tools, which may include blood work, imaging studies, or biopsies
- Discuss treatment options tailored to your dog's specific case, potentially involving surgery, chemotherapy, radiation therapy, or a combination of approaches
- Consider integrative therapies to support overall health and manage side effects, such as acupuncture or herbal supplements, under veterinary guidance
- Implement palliative care strategies to ensure comfort and quality of life in advanced cases, focusing on pain

management and emotional well-being

- Maintain open communication with your veterinary team to adjust the care plan as needed, ensuring it aligns with your dog's changing needs and your family's goals

7. Sensory Decline: Navigating Vision and Hearing Changes in Senior Dogs

As dogs age, their sensory capabilities often diminish, particularly in the realms of vision and hearing. Recognizing and adapting to these changes is crucial for maintaining your senior dog's quality of life and safety.

Signs of Sensory Decline:

- Frequent collisions with furniture or walls, especially in dim lighting or rearranged spaces
- Diminished responsiveness to vocal commands or environmental sounds
- Increased startle reflex when approached or touched unexpectedly
- Difficulty locating toys or treats, even when nearby
- Hesitation on stairs or when navigating unfamiliar terrain

Management:

- Maintain a consistent home layout, minimizing frequent furniture rearrangements
- Incorporate hand signals and visual cues for dogs with hearing loss
- Use scent markers or textured mats to help visually impaired dogs navigate key areas
- Ensure adequate lighting, especially on stairs and in dimly lit corners
- Approach your dog gently and predictably to avoid startling them

- Consider using bells or vibration collars for dogs with significant hearing loss
- Consult with your veterinarian about potential supplements or treatments to support eye and ear health

Emotional Needs: The Heart of Senior Care

As your canine companion enters their golden years, their emotional needs may evolve, requiring additional support and understanding. Here are some key aspects to consider when providing emotional care for your ageing dog:

- Patience and Understanding: Your senior dog may develop new limitations or exhibit changes in behavior. Approach these changes with empathy and patience, allowing them time to adjust and adapt.
- Gentle and Consistent Handling: Older dogs may become more sensitive to touch or startle easily. Employ gentle, predictable handling techniques to help them feel secure and comfortable in their interactions with you.
- Calm and Serene Environments: Create peaceful spaces within your home where your senior dog can relax and feel at ease. Minimize loud noises and sudden disturbances to reduce stress and anxiety.
- Increased Affection and Bonding Time: Your ageing companion may seek more comfort and reassurance. Dedicate extra time for gentle cuddles, soft petting, and quiet companionship to strengthen your bond and provide emotional support.
- Routine and Stability: Establish and maintain consistent daily routines to provide a sense of security and predict-

ability for your senior dog, helping to alleviate any confusion or anxiety they may experience.

Hospice and End-of-Life Care: Compassion in the Final Days

As we approach the final chapter of our beloved senior dog's life, it becomes crucial to understand and prepare for end-of-life care. While this topic may be emotionally challenging, it is an essential aspect of responsible senior dog ownership that allows us to provide comfort, dignity, and love during our furry friend's twilight years:

1. Vigilantly monitoring your dog's overall well-being and recognizing subtle changes that may indicate a decline in their quality of life, such as persistent pain, loss of appetite, or difficulty performing daily activities
2. Collaborating closely with your veterinarian to develop a comprehensive pain management strategy, which may include medications, alternative therapies, and environmental modifications to ensure your dog's comfort and minimize discomfort
3. Educating yourself about various end-of-life care options, including hospice care and different methods of euthanasia, such as at-home services that can provide a peaceful and familiar environment for your dog's final moments
4. Taking time to process your emotions, seek support from loved ones or pet loss support groups, and create lasting memories with your canine companion through gentle activities, photography, or special outings tailored to their current abilities

5. Discussing end-of-life decisions with family members to ensure everyone is on the same page and can provide a united front of love and support for your ageing dog

Making the difficult decision to say goodbye is ultimately an act of profound love and compassion when it serves to prevent unnecessary suffering and honors the quality of life your faithful companion deserves. This final gift allows us to prioritize our dog's well-being above our own desire to keep them with us, ensuring their journey ends with dignity and peace.

The Joy of Senior Dogs: A Perspective Shift

Caring for a senior dog brings special rewards that make both your lives richer. After years together, you develop a deep connection where you can understand each other without words - just a look can say everything. Your older dog becomes a gentle, calming presence in your home, offering comfort during both good and difficult times.

As your dog slows down, you begin to appreciate the quiet moments more - like their peaceful sighs, gentle tail wags, or afternoon naps together. This experience can also teach valuable lessons to children about caring and the natural cycle of life. Most importantly, the love of a senior dog shows us what true devotion means. Their loyalty, shaped by years of shared experiences, remains strong regardless of their age or physical changes.

Understanding and embracing your dog's ageing process allows you to provide the best care and enjoy this special time together. Remember, ageing is not a disease – it's a natural part of life that can be beautiful when approached with knowledge, patience, and love.

Your senior dog has given you years of loyalty, love, and joy. Now is your time to return that love with gentle care, understanding, and appreciation for every precious moment you share. The gray muzzle, the slow walks, the quiet companionship – these are not signs of a diminished relationship, but of one that has deepened and matured like fine wine.

Cherish these golden years, for they are filled with a unique beauty all their own. Your senior dog may move a little slower, but their capacity for love remains as boundless as ever.

15. Final Words

As we come to the end of this book, it's evident that the journey of dog ownership is one of continuous learning, adaptability, and boundless love. From the exciting days of welcoming a new puppy into your home to the gentle care of a senior dog, each stage of your dog's life brings its own joys, challenges, and opportunities for deepening your bond.

As any dog owner will attest, welcoming a canine companion into your life is a profoundly transformative experience that touches every aspect of your daily existence. Dogs possess an extraordinary and almost magical ability to reshape our lives in ways both subtle and dramatic. Their impact on our emotional, physical, and social well-being cannot be overstated. Let's explore some of the remarkable ways in which dogs enrich our lives:

- Teach us patience and unconditional love: Dogs have an uncanny knack for testing our patience, whether it's through their occasional mischief or their need for consistent training. Yet, through these challenges, they also demonstrate an unwavering, unconditional love that serves as a powerful lesson in acceptance and affection.
- Encourage us to be more active and engaged with the world around us: The need for regular walks and playtime

not only benefits our furry friends but also motivates us to lead more active lifestyles. Dogs inspire us to explore our surroundings, breathe fresh air, and appreciate the simple joys of nature, fostering a deeper connection with our environment.

- Provide comfort during difficult times: In moments of stress, sadness, or anxiety, dogs seem to possess an innate ability to sense our emotional state. Their presence alone can be incredibly soothing, offering a silent but powerful support system that helps us navigate life's challenges with greater resilience.
- Bring laughter and joy into our daily lives: From their silly antics to their enthusiastic greetings, dogs have an unparalleled talent for infusing our days with moments of pure joy and laughter. Their playful nature serves as a constant reminder to find happiness in the little things and not take life too seriously.
- Connect us with other dog lovers, building a sense of community: Dog ownership opens doors to a vibrant community of fellow animal enthusiasts. Whether it's striking up conversations at the dog park, participating in training classes, or joining online forums, dogs facilitate connections that can blossom into meaningful friendships and a strong support network.

The beauty of the human-canine relationship lies in its reciprocal nature. As we dedicate ourselves to caring for our dogs, providing them with love, attention, and the necessities of life, we often discover that they, in turn, care for us with equal, if not greater, devotion. Their unwavering loyalty, intuitive understanding of our emotions, and constant companionship create a bond that goes beyond mere pet ownership, evolving into a profound partnership that enriches both human and canine lives in immeasurable ways.

We have emphasized this point throughout the book, but

it bears repeating: the concept of lifelong commitment is often underestimated by potential dog owners. Time and again, we have encountered situations where individuals fail to fully comprehend the extent of this dedication. It's crucial to understand that your canine companion depends on you entirely for their well-being and happiness. This encompasses not just the basics of survival – such as providing nutritious food and a safe, comfortable shelter – but also extends to ensuring their physical health through regular veterinary care, maintaining their mental and physical stimulation through exercise and play, and nurturing their emotional needs with consistent love and attention.

This commitment is undoubtedly demanding, requiring a significant investment of time, energy, and resources. It may involve sacrificing personal conveniences, adjusting your lifestyle, and making decisions with your dog's needs in mind. However, it's important to recognize that this dedication is not without its rewards. The returns on this investment are immeasurable and often exceed our expectations. Your unwavering commitment is reciprocated manifold in the form of your dog's steadfast loyalty, their unbridled affection, and their constant companionship. The bond that develops between a devoted owner and their dog is truly special, offering a depth of connection that enriches our lives in countless ways.

As our understanding of canine behaviour, health, and cognition continues to advance through ongoing research and scientific studies, it is inevitable that our approaches to dog care will evolve alongside this growing knowledge base. The field of canine science is dynamic and ever-expanding, with new insights emerging regularly that challenge our preconceptions and refine our understanding of our four-legged companions.

As responsible dog owners, it is incumbent upon us to remain intellectually curious and receptive to these developments. We must cultivate a mindset of lifelong learning when it comes to dog care, constantly seeking out new information, staying abreast of the latest findings in veterinary medicine, animal behavior, and nutrition. This commitment to ongoing education enables us to adapt our care practices, ensuring that we are always providing the best possible support for our canine friends. By maintaining an open mind and a willingness to incorporate new, evidence-based practices into our routines, we can significantly enhance our dogs' overall well-being, longevity, and quality of life.

So, as you close this book and look into your dog's eyes, know that you're part of something truly special. Whether you're just starting out on your dog ownership journey or you're a seasoned pet parent, each day with your dog is a gift. Cherish it, learn from it, and most of all, enjoy the incredible journey of life with your canine best friend.

Acknowledgements

Writing this book has been both a joy and a journey of discovery. This work would not have been possible without the support, knowledge, and inspiration of many individuals who share a deep love for our canine companions.

First and foremost, I want to express my profound gratitude to the countless dogs who have touched my life and taught me invaluable lessons about love, patience, and the pure joy of living in the moment. Special thanks to Karan Mahendru, my constant companion and inspiration throughout this writing journey.

I am deeply indebted to the veterinary professionals, dog trainers and behaviorists, and animal shelter and rescue organizations who generously shared their expertise and insights.

Special thanks to my fellow dog owners and pet parents who shared their personal stories, experiences, and photographs, adding depth and authenticity to this guide. Your openness about both the joys and challenges of dog ownership has made this book richer and more relatable.

I am particularly grateful to my parents, who instilled in me a love for animals from an early age. Their support and encouragement have been instrumental in shaping both my career and my passion for pet care. A special thanks to my brother, whose own experiences with pets have provided valuable insights and perspectives that have enriched this book. I am deeply indebted to my wife and children, who have shown incredible patience and understanding during the many long nights spent developing this book. Their unwavering support and encouragement made this work possible, and I could not have completed it without their love and understanding.

A special acknowledgment to Sarthak Ahuja for pushing me to start working on this idea and connecting me to Yashraj and the team at Wyzr. I am indebted to him for his invaluable business insights and enthusiastic support.

The online pet care communities and forums whose members share their experiences and support one another in their journey of dog ownership—your collective wisdom has been an invaluable resource.

To the researchers and scientists who continue to advance our understanding of canine health, behaviour, and the human-animal bond—your work forms the foundation of modern dog care practices.

To my editing and publishing team, Wyzr:

- Yashraj Sharma, for his meticulous attention to detail and bringing a non-pet parent perspective to all the chapters we conceived
- Amlan Chakravarty, for editing the rough drafts and notes into the book you now hold in your hands, and adding his perspective as a dog parent of seven years
- The entire team at Wyzr, for believing in this project

Finally, my deepest gratitude goes to you, the readers, who have chosen to embark on or continue your journey of dog ownership and have placed your faith in this book as your guide. Your commitment to providing the best possible care for your canine companions makes the world a better place for dogs and humans alike.

Explore other titles by Wyzr

About the author

Akshay is the co-founder and CEO of The Pet Point, a leading pet store chain in North India. He's also the co-founder of Nootie, a pet care brand known for its innovative, clinically proven grooming products.

Akshay has been a dog parent for over two decades and, through his work, has touched the lives of countless pets and their families. His successful businesses are an outcome of his love for pets. He's a staunch advocate for responsible pet ownership and holistic pet care, and this book is another attempt to promote that.

11/07/25

p.